Art

By

Santo

Broken Talent and

TPOS

mANGROVe

roots

Ative

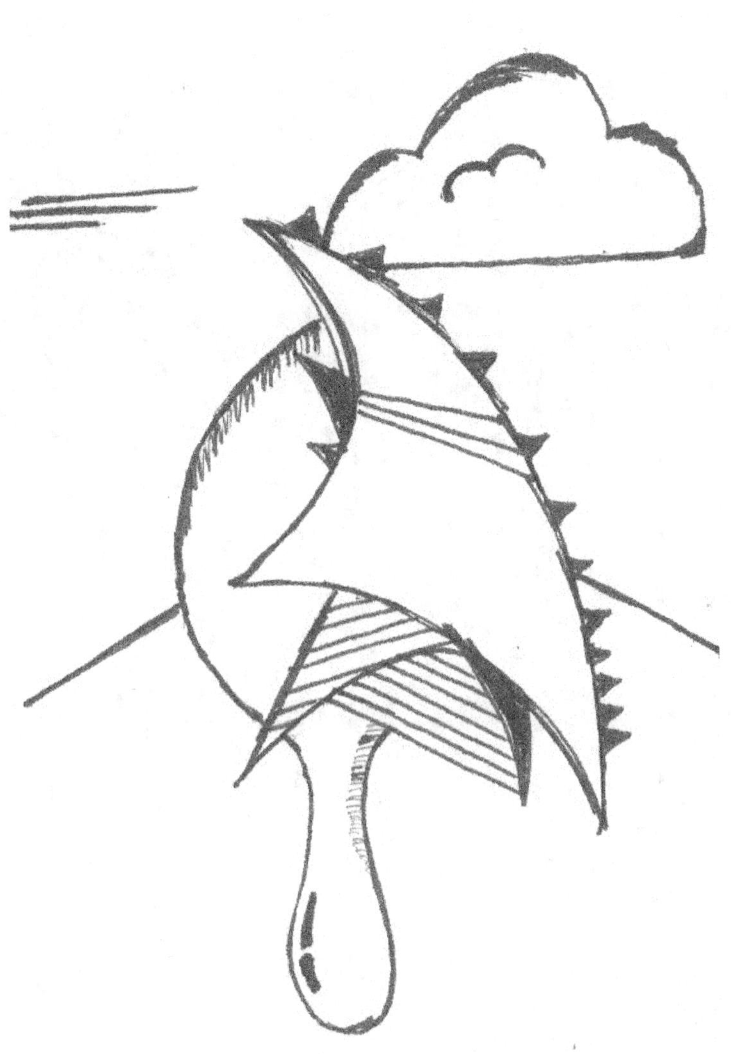

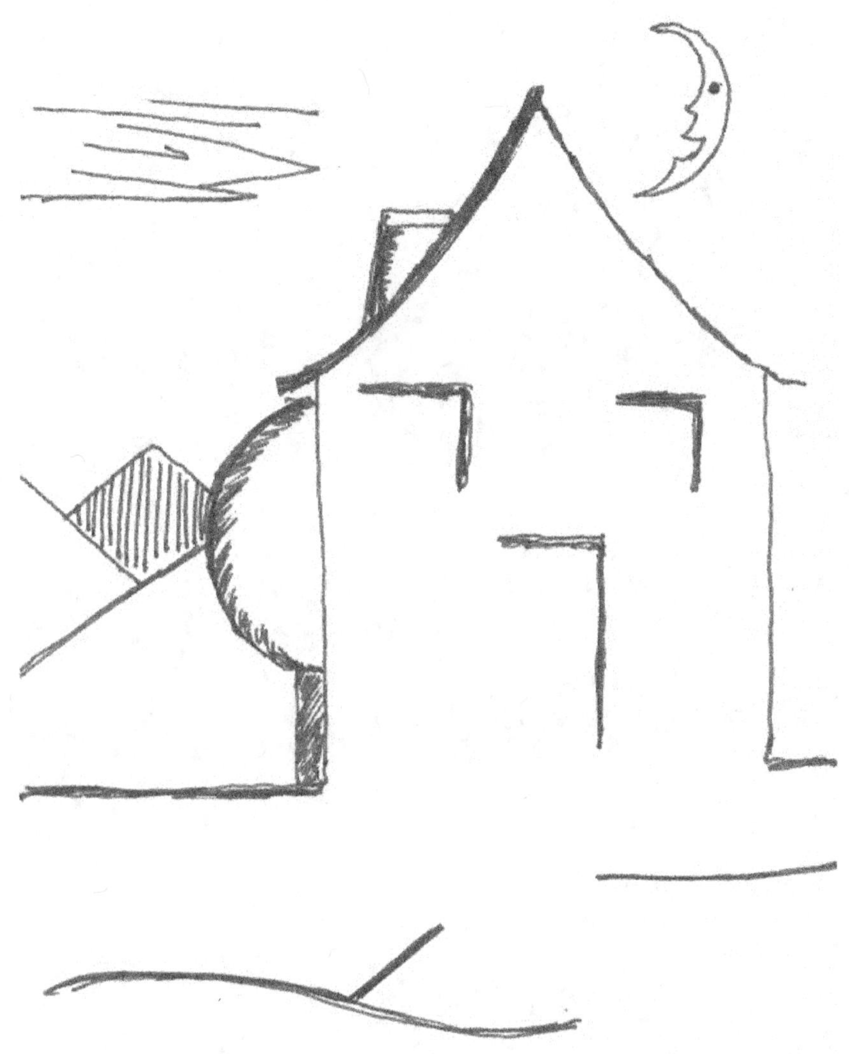

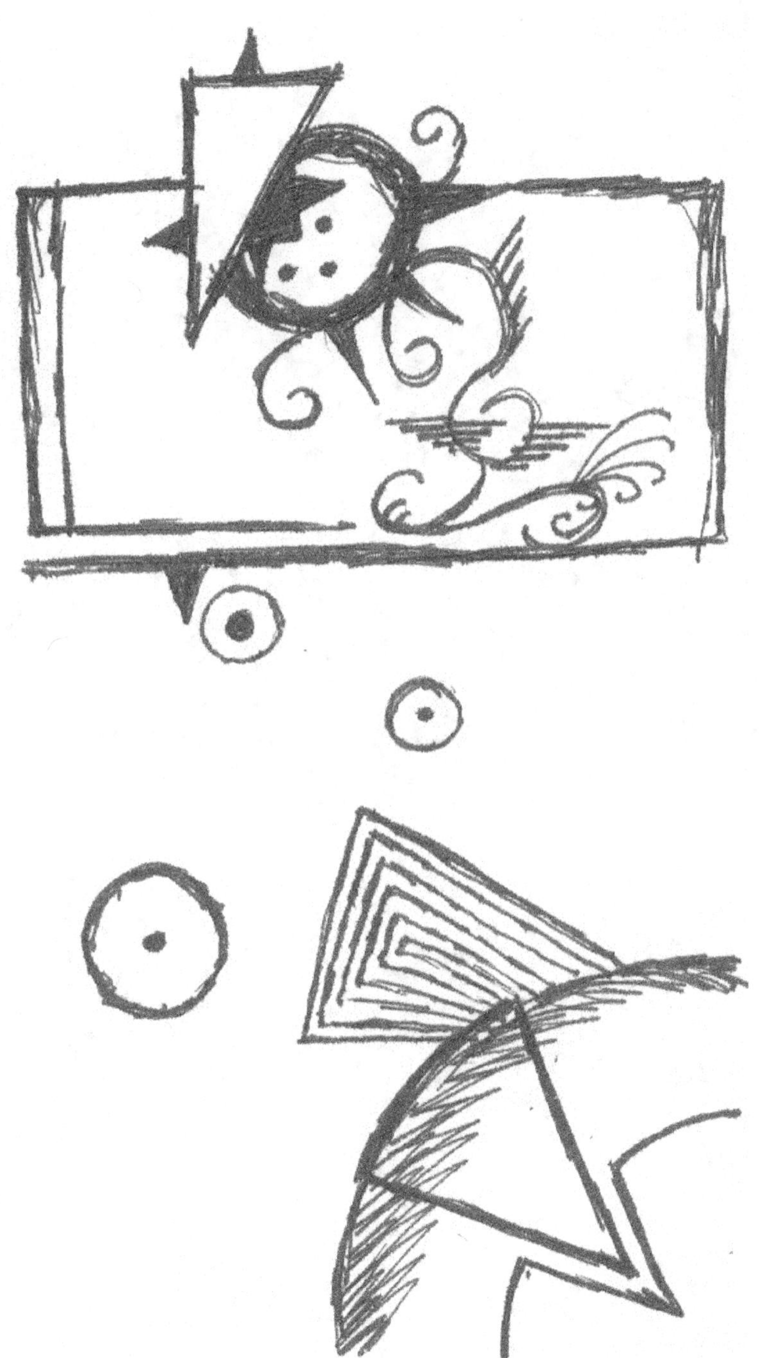

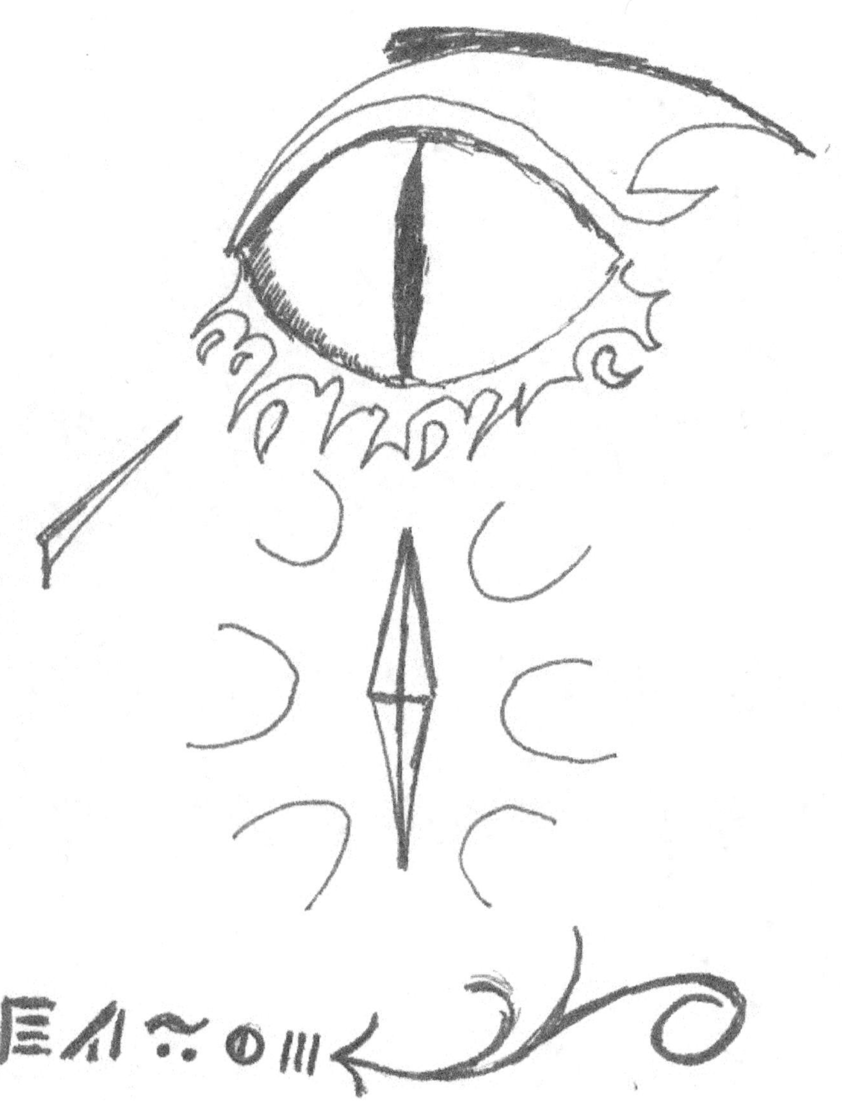

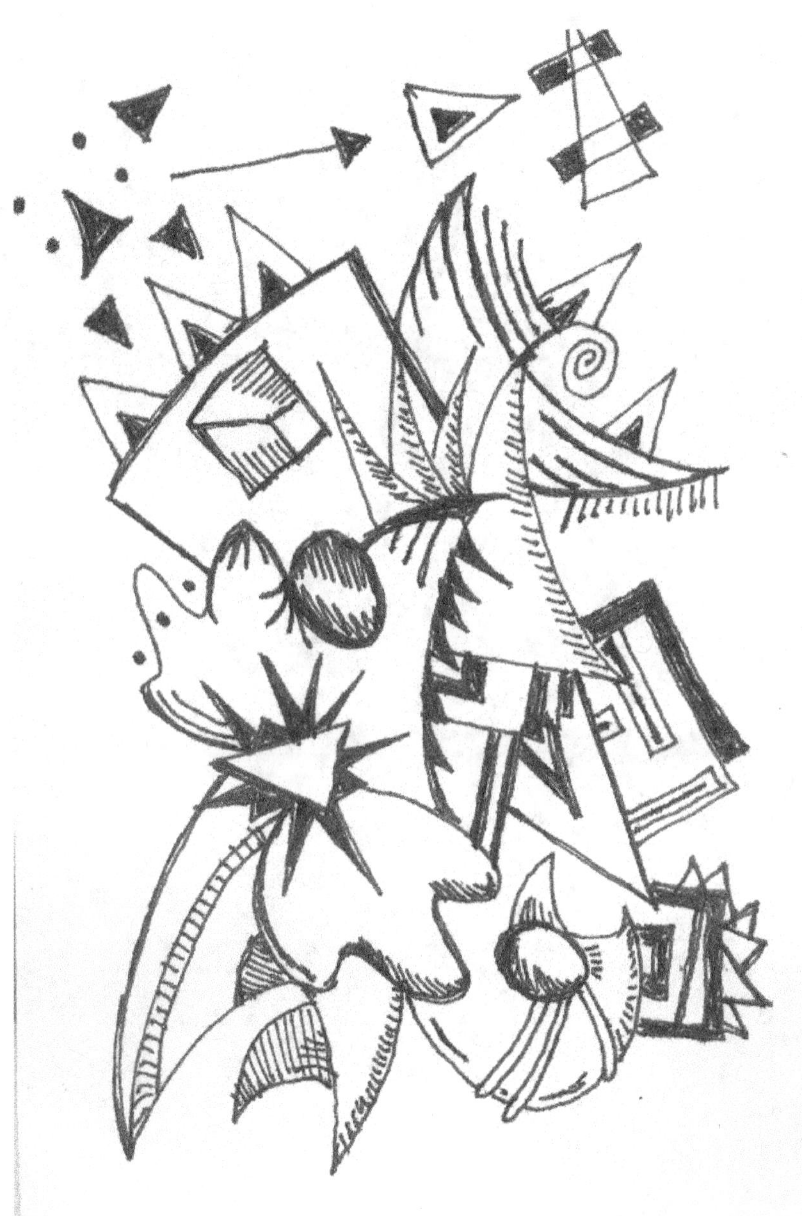

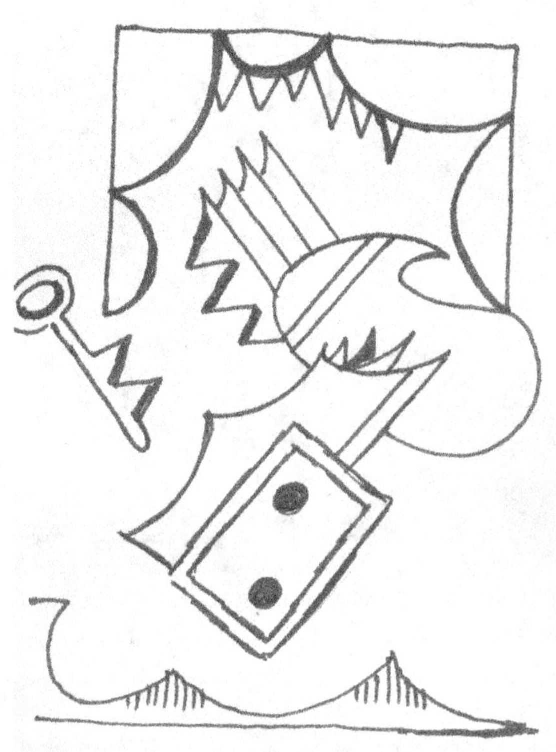

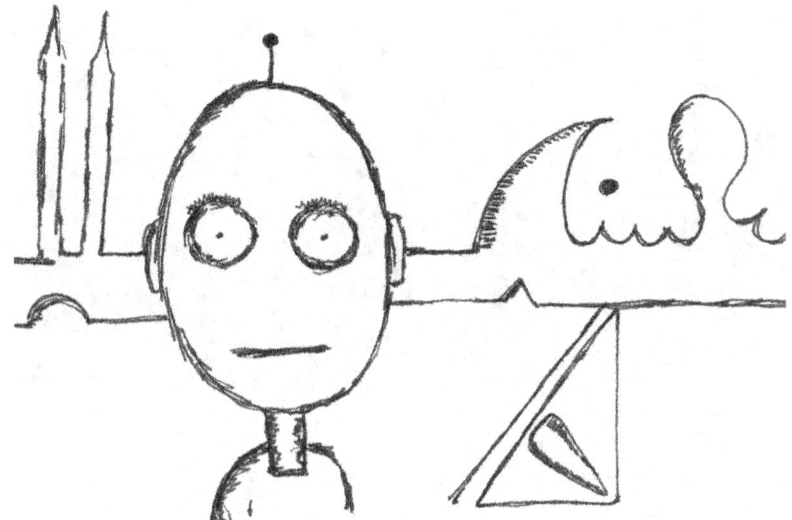

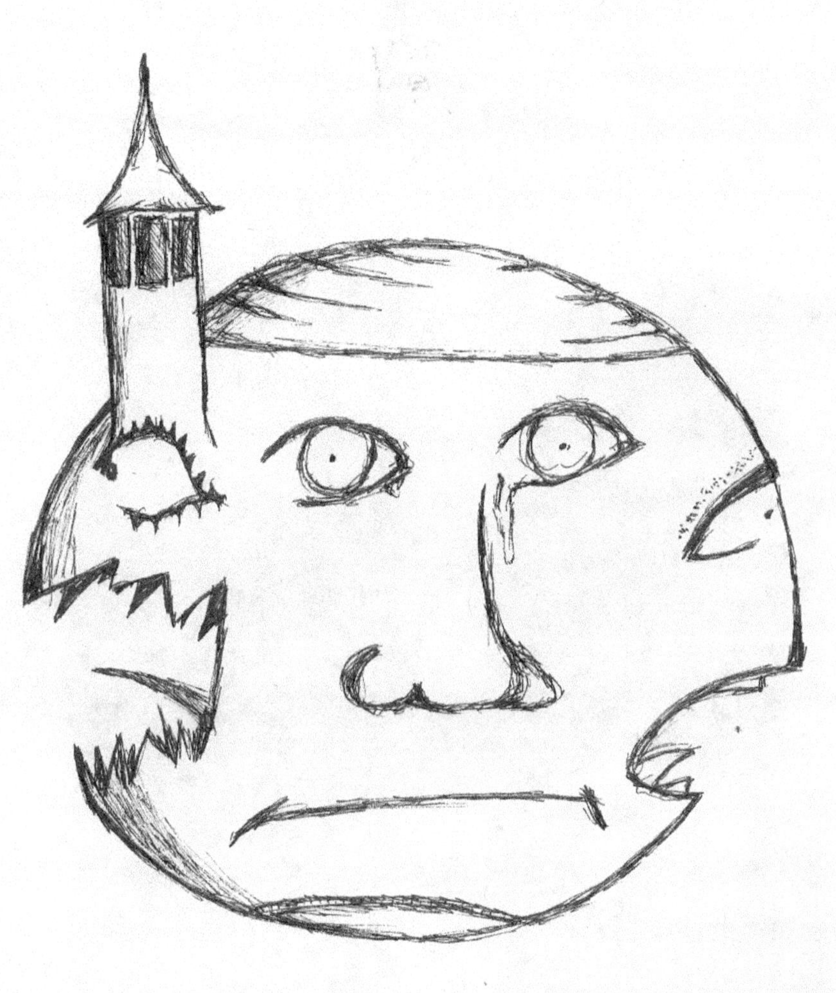

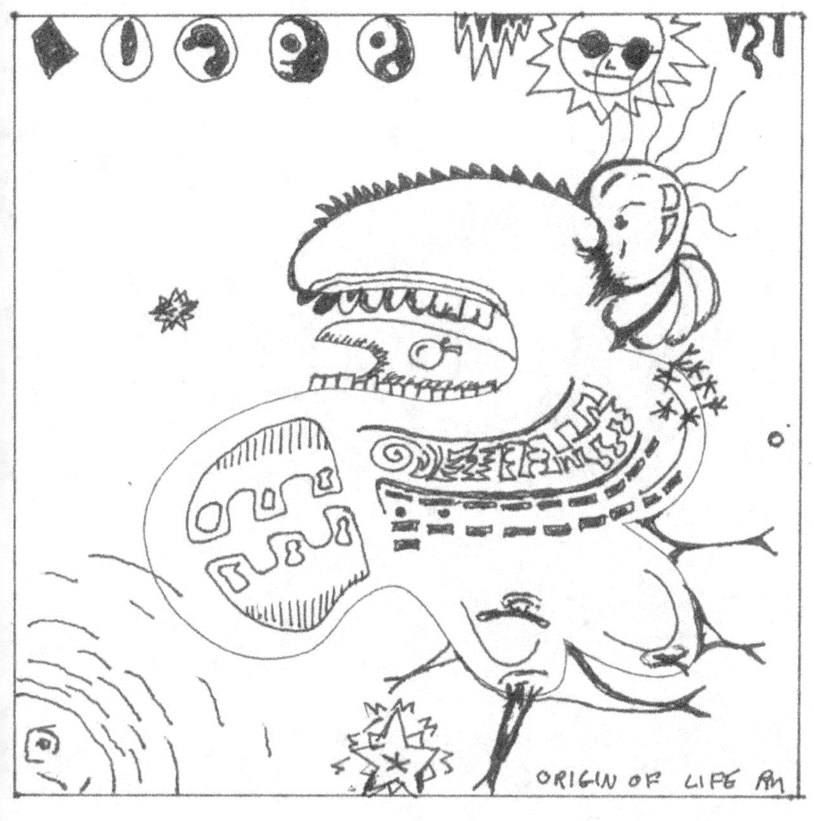

Energy into the system
Everything has a pattern and it may
    seem disorganized and the reason
may be the magnification of perspective

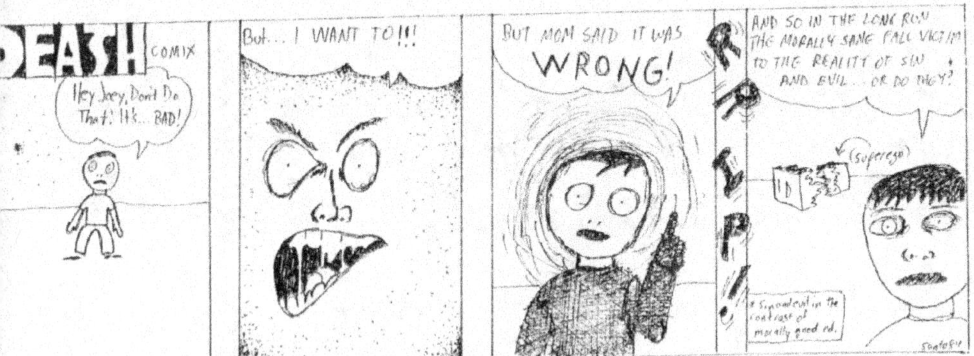

DEATH! COMIX
Hey Joey, Don't Do That! It's... BAD!
But... I WANT TO!!!
BUT MOM SAID IT WAS WRONG!
RRIPP!
AND SO IN THE LONG RUN THE MORALLY SANE FALL VICTIM TO THE REALITY OF SIN AND EVIL... OR DO THEY?
(superego)
* Signosdent in the contrast of morally good ed.

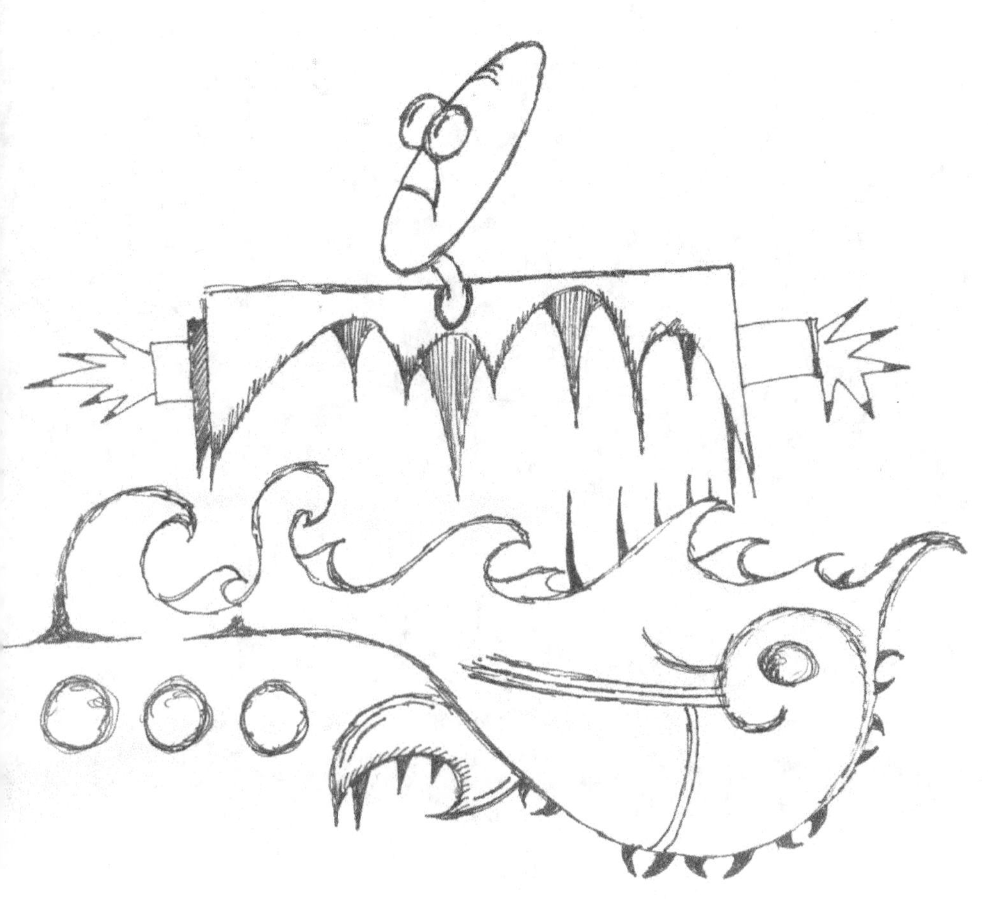

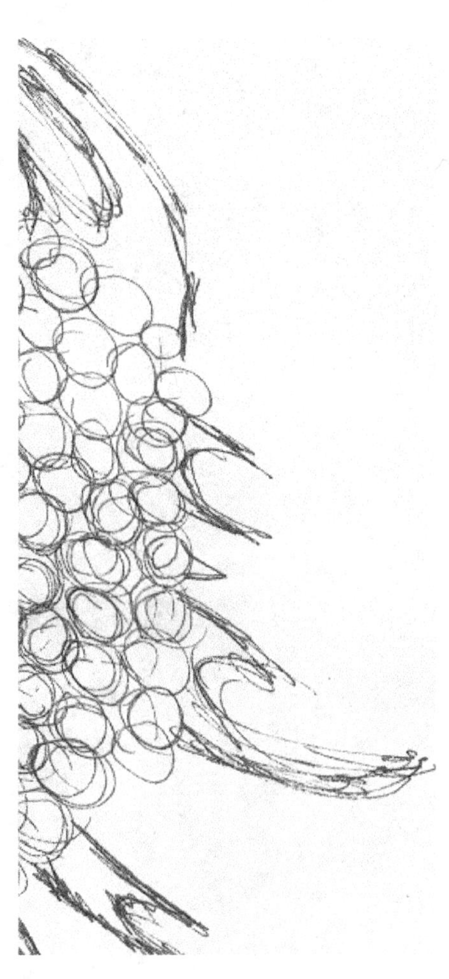

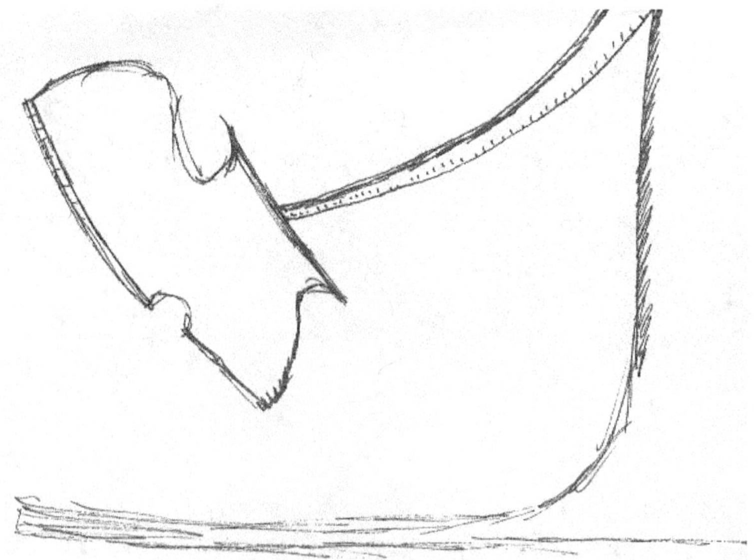

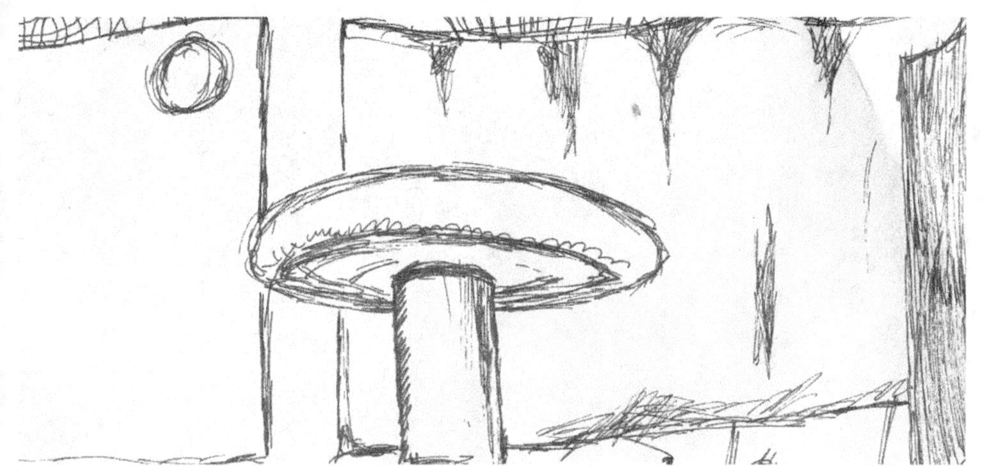

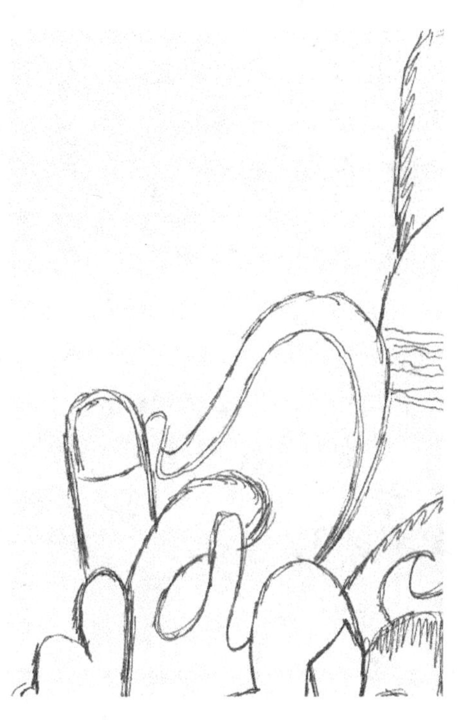

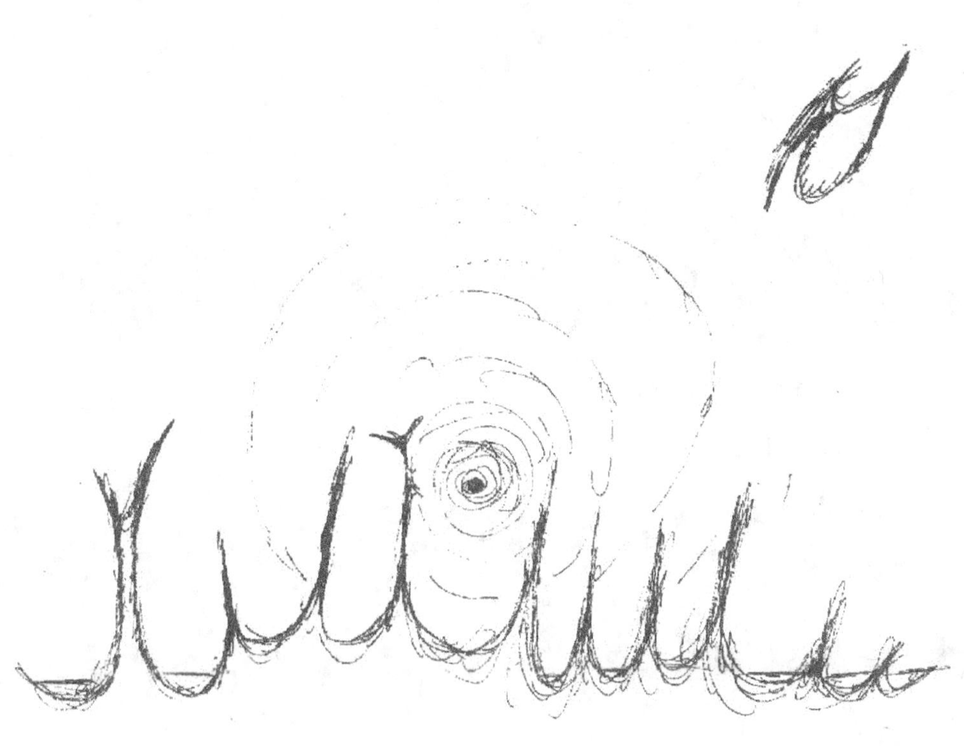

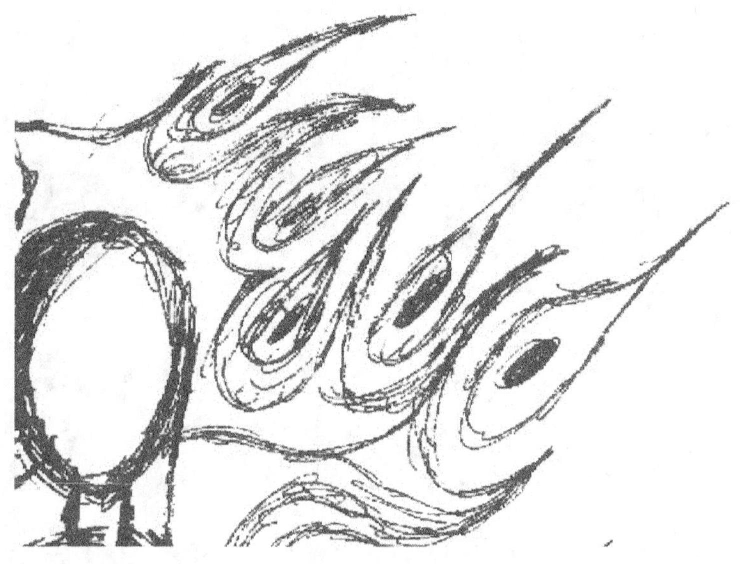

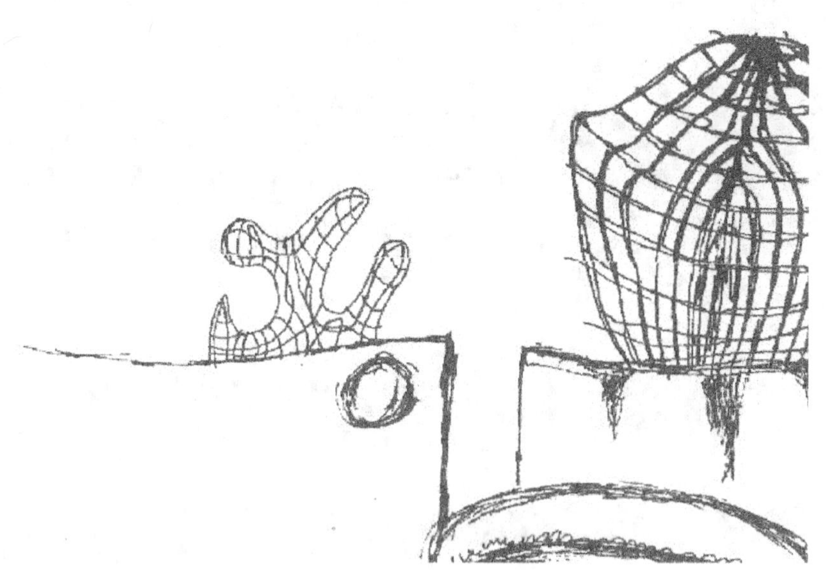

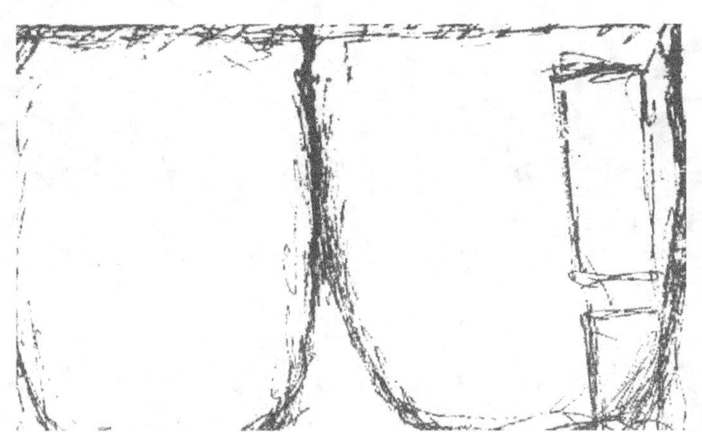

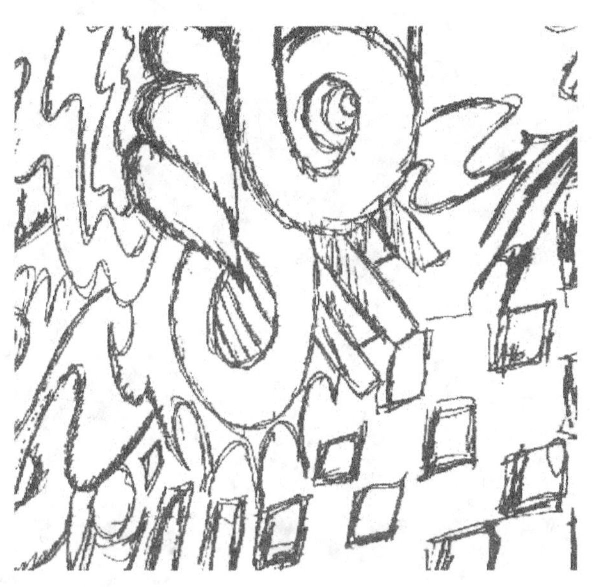

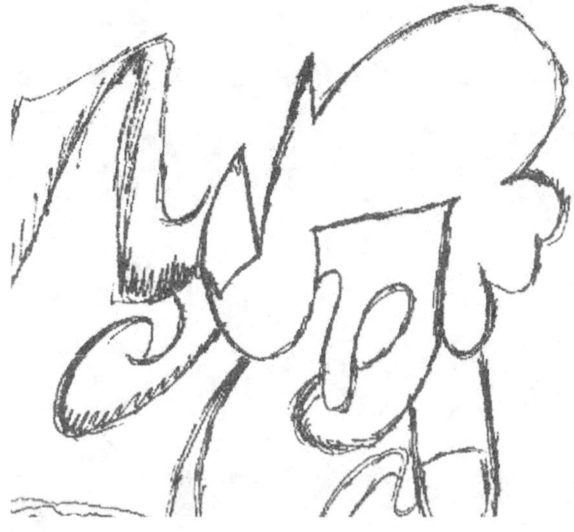

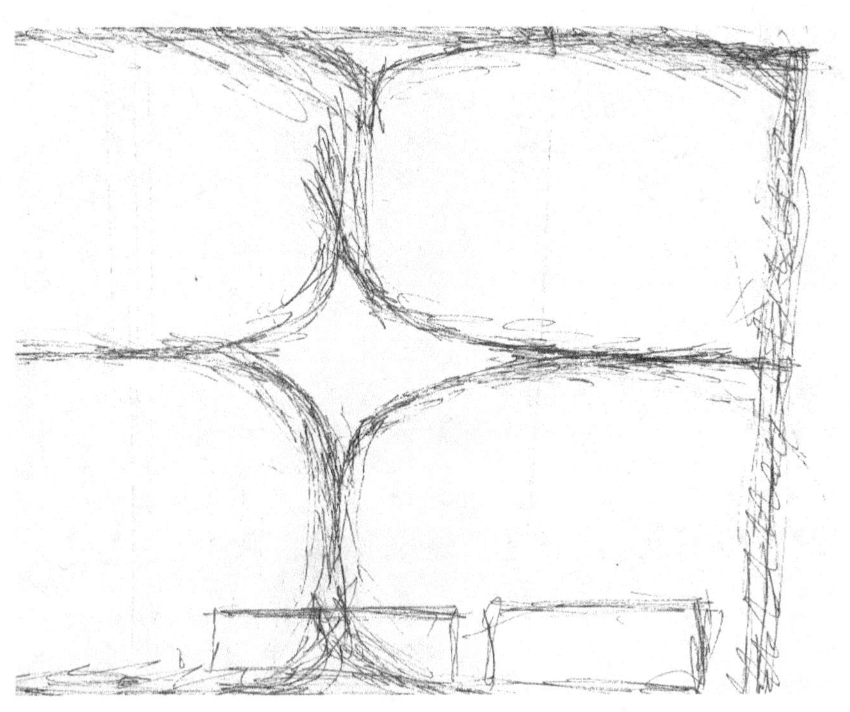

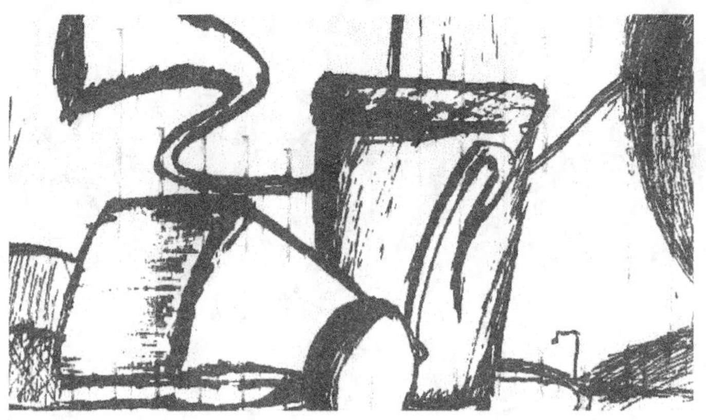

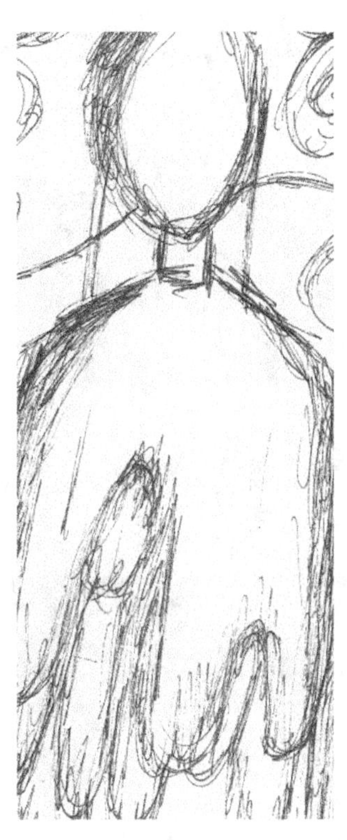

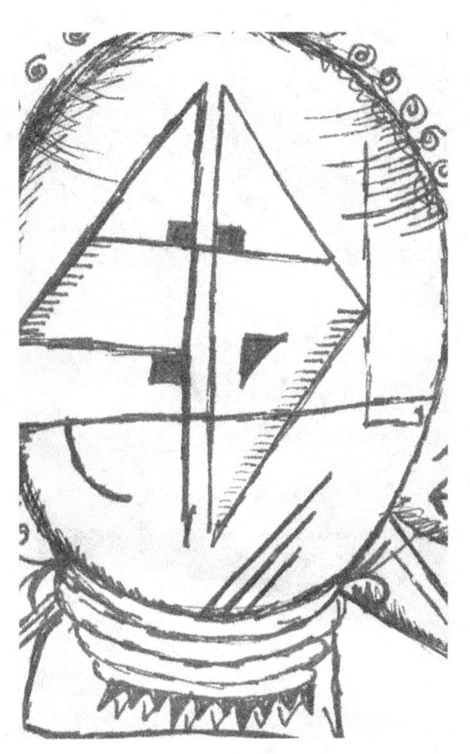

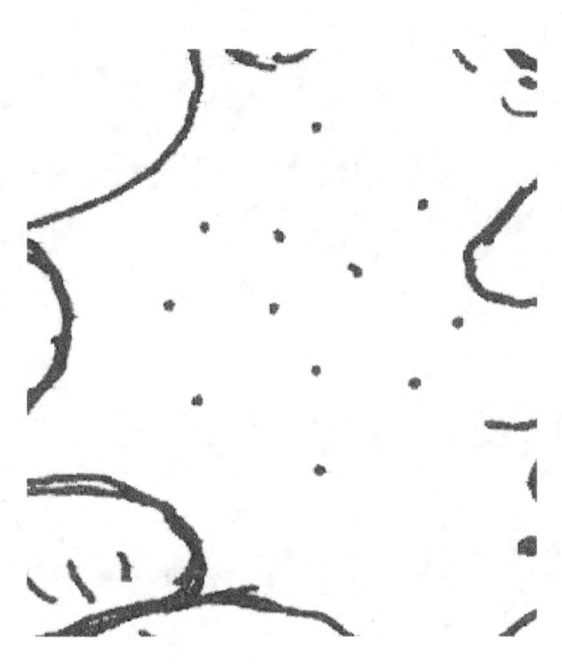

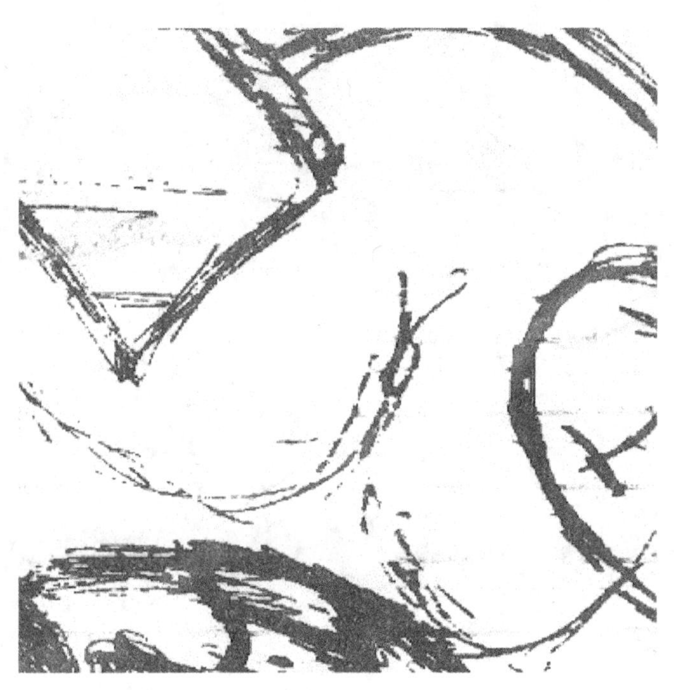

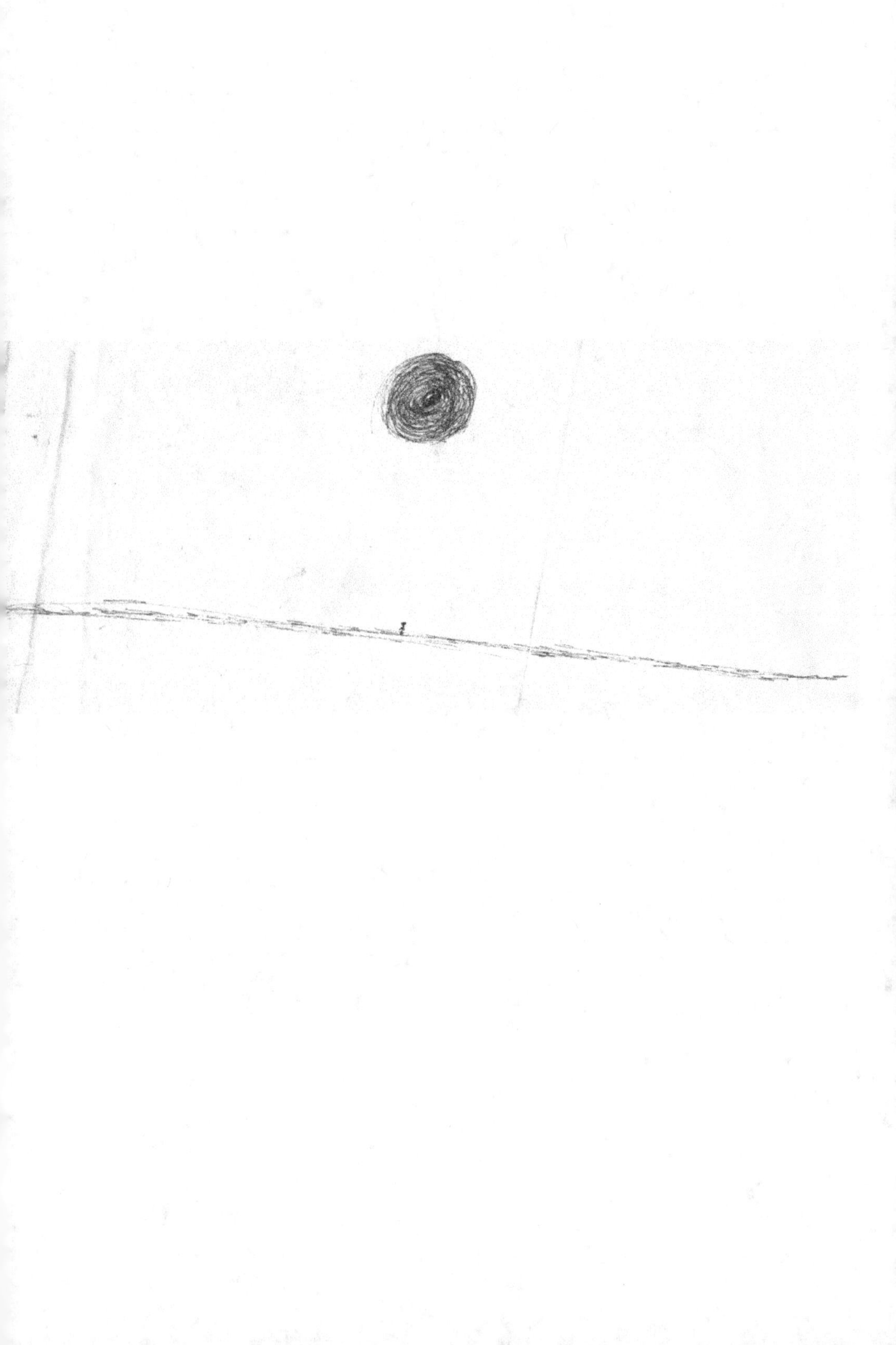

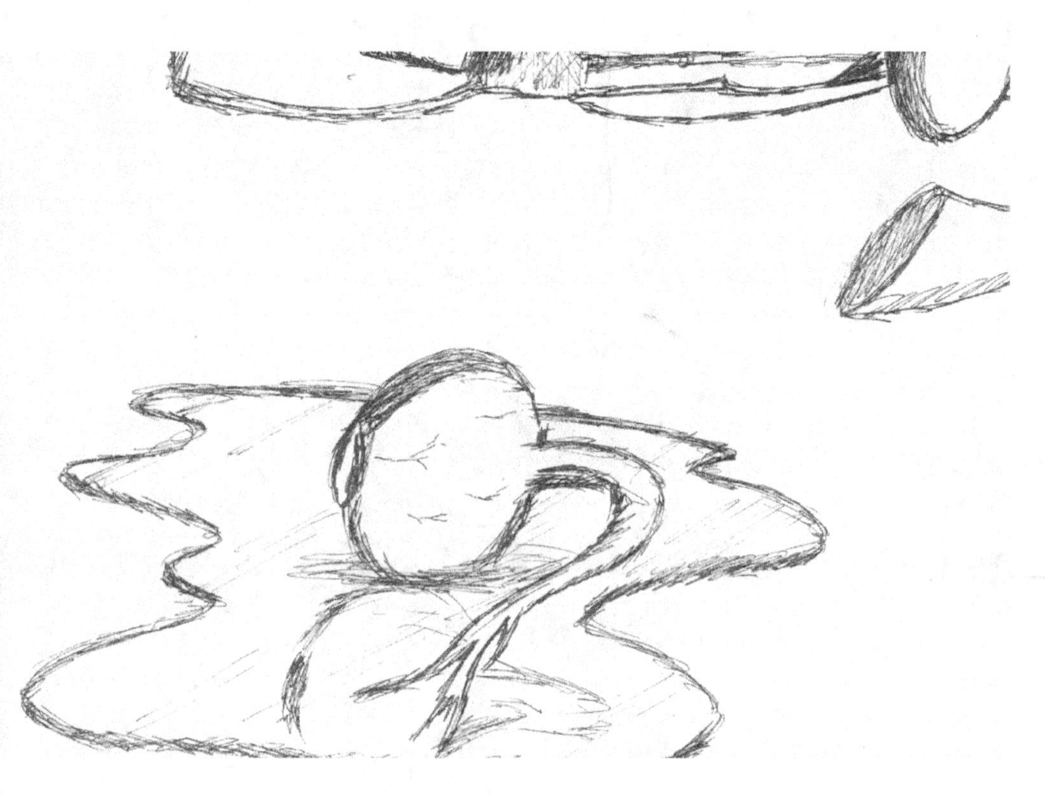

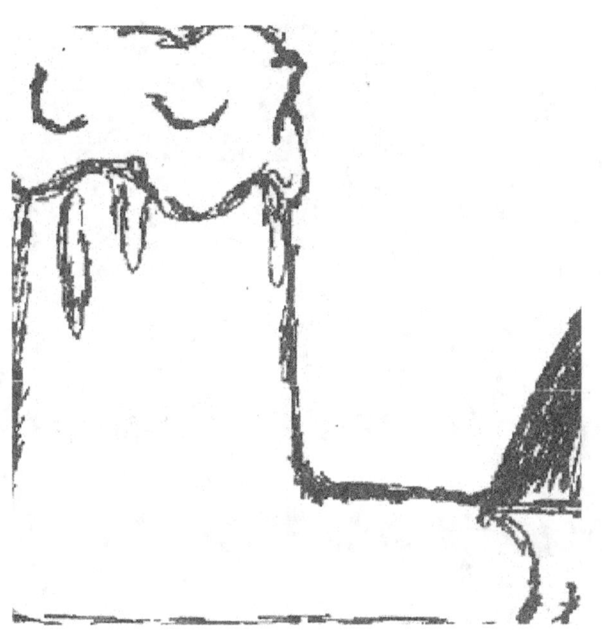

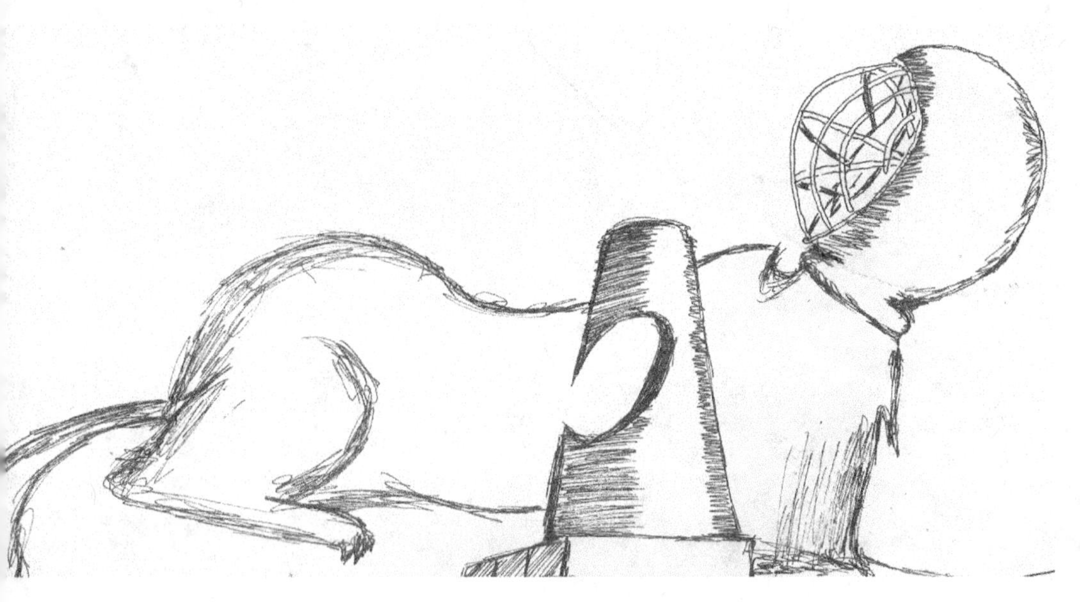

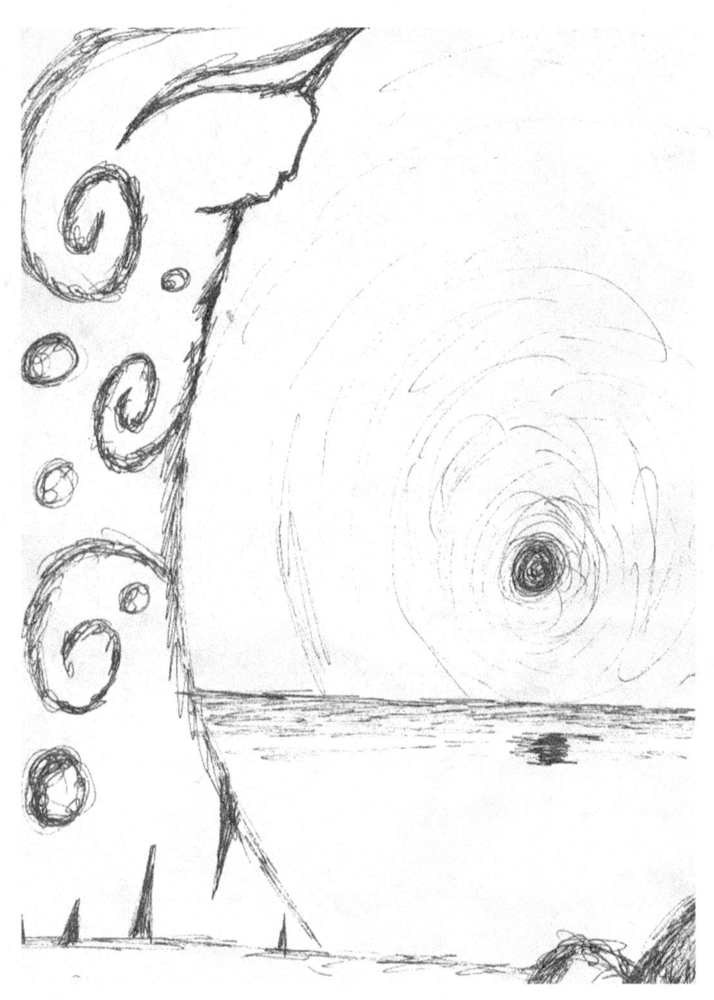

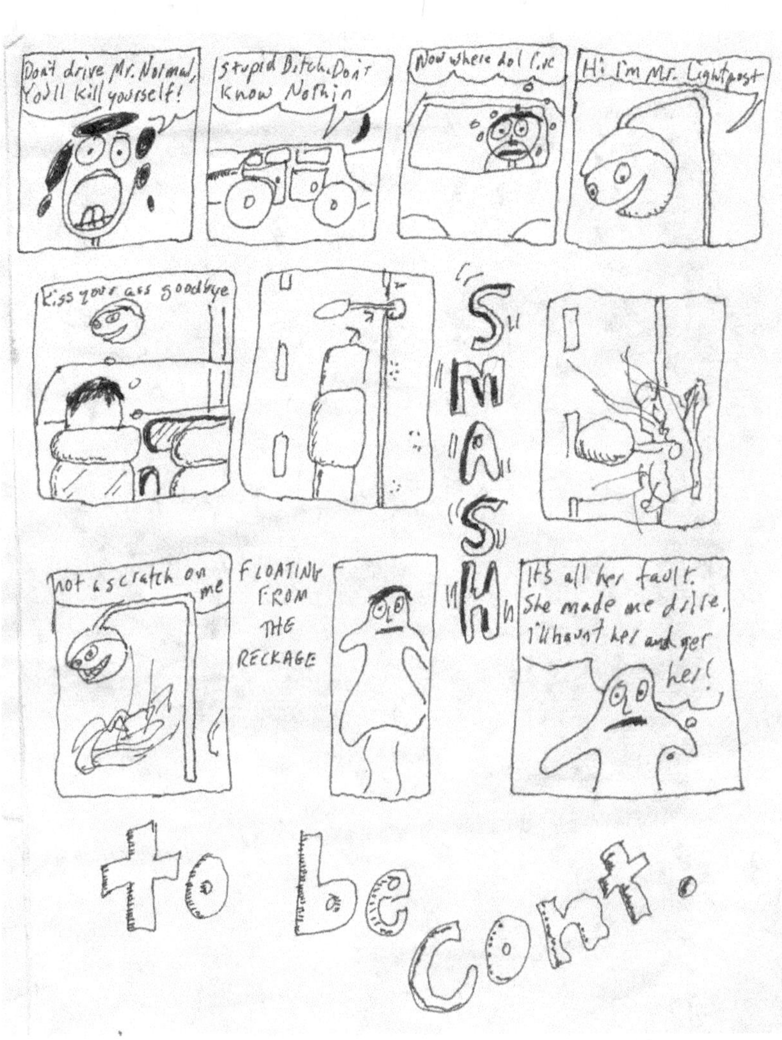
Don't drive Mr. Normal, you'll kill yourself!
Stupid Bitch. Don't know Nothin
Now where do I live
Hi I'm Mr. Lightpost
Kiss your ass goodbye
"SMASH"
not a scratch on me
FLOATING FROM THE RECKAGE
It's all her fault. She made me dizze. I'll haunt her and get her!
to be cont.

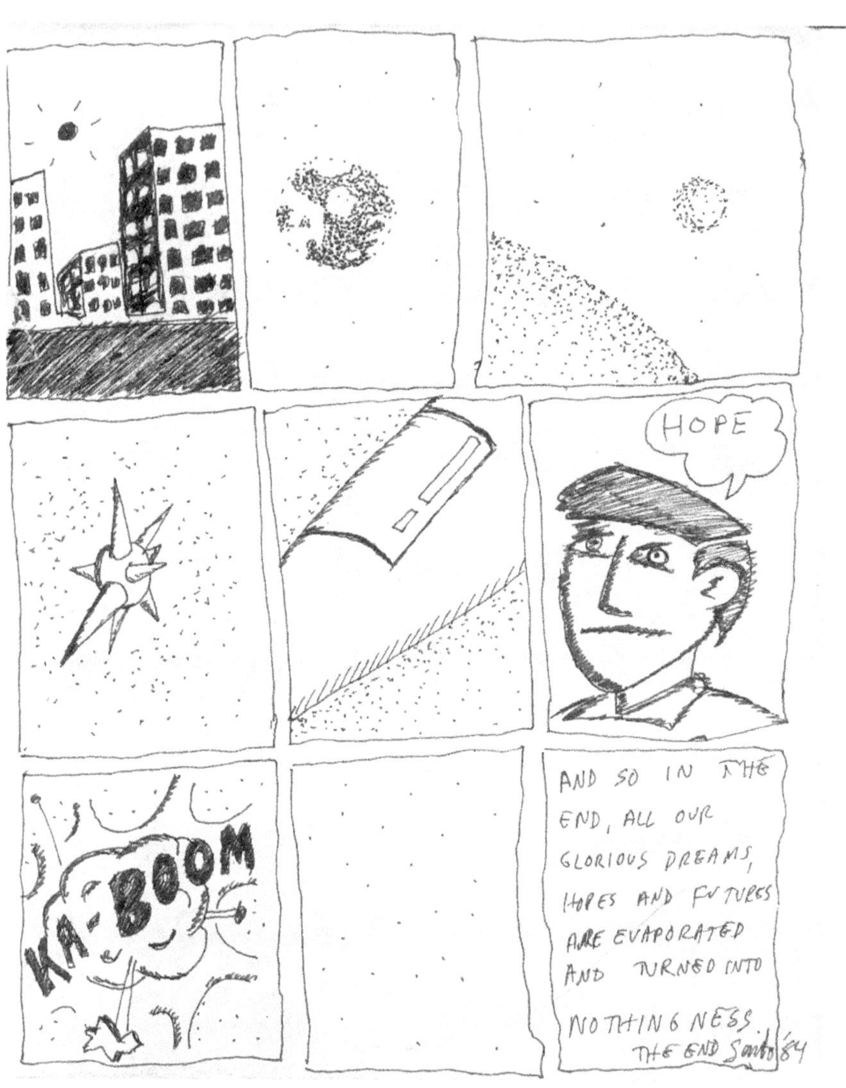

HOPE
KA-BOOM
AND SO IN THE END, ALL OUR GLORIOUS DREAMS, HOPES AND FUTURES ARE EVAPORATED AND TURNED INTO NOTHINGNESS.
THE END Santo '84

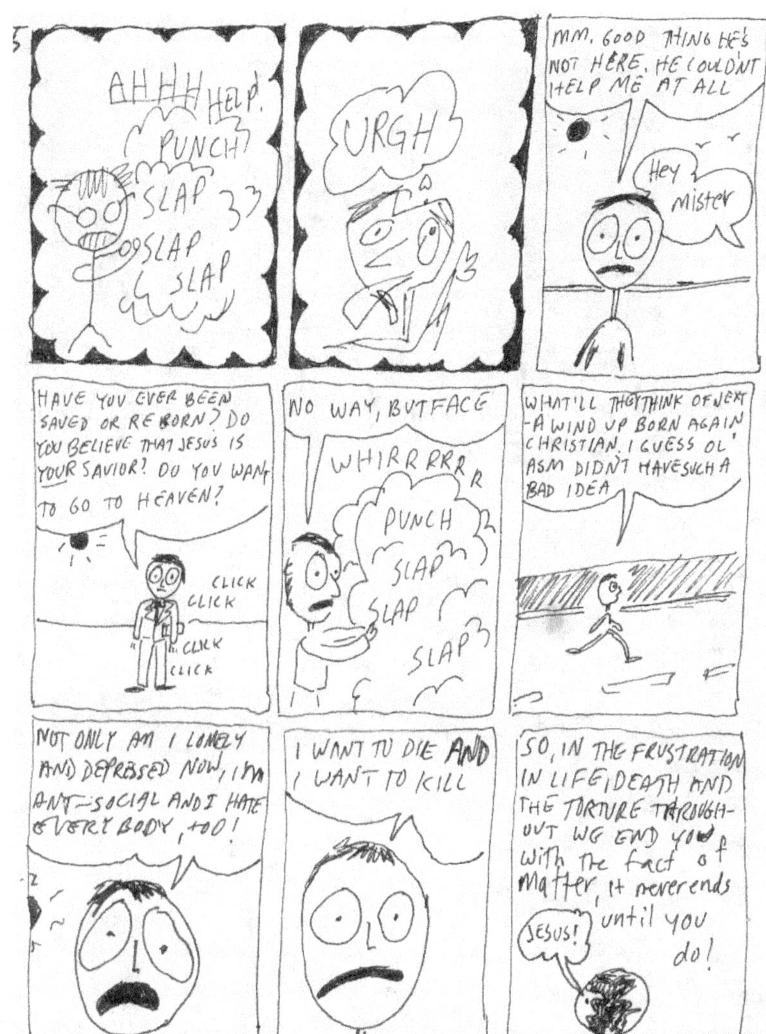

AHHH HELP!
PUNCH
SLAP
SLAP
SLAP
URGH
MM. GOOD THING HE'S NOT HERE, HE COULDN'T HELP ME AT ALL
Hey mister
HAVE YOU EVER BEEN SAVED OR REBORN? DO YOU BELIEVE THAT JESUS IS YOUR SAVIOR? DO YOU WANT TO GO TO HEAVEN?
CLICK CLICK
CLICK CLICK
NO WAY, BUTFACE
WHIRRRRR
PUNCH
SLAP
SLAP
SLAP
WHAT'LL THEY THINK OF NEXT - A WIND UP BORN AGAIN CHRISTIAN. I GUESS OL' ASM DIDN'T HAVE SUCH A BAD IDEA
NOT ONLY AM I LONELY AND DEPRESSED NOW, I'M ANTI-SOCIAL AND I HATE EVERYBODY, too!
I WANT TU DIE AND I WANT TO KILL
SO, IN THE FRUSTRATION IN LIFE, DEATH AND THE TORTURE THROUGHOUT WE END YOU WITH THE FACT OF MATTER, it never ends until you do!
JESUS!

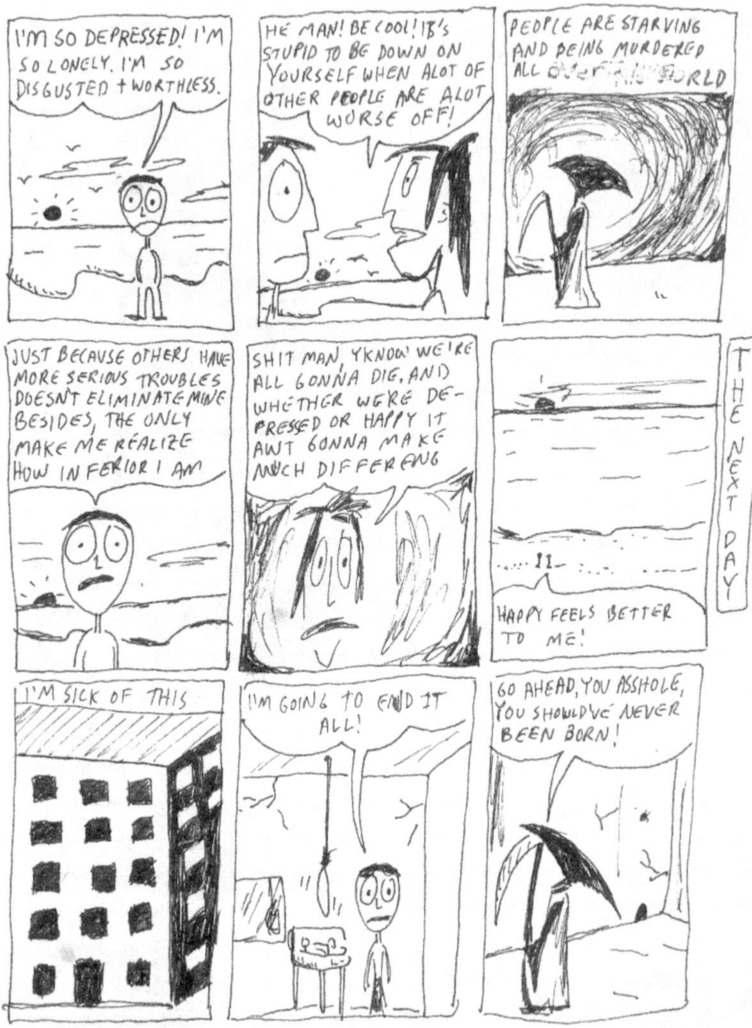

I'M SO DEPRESSED! I'M SO LONELY. I'M SO DISGUSTED + WORTHLESS.
HE MAN! BE COOL! IT'S STUPID TO BE DOWN ON YOURSELF WHEN ALOT OF OTHER PEOPLE ARE ALOT WORSE OFF!
PEOPLE ARE STARVING AND BEING MURDERED ALL OVER THE WORLD
JUST BECAUSE OTHERS HAVE MORE SERIOUS TROUBLES DOESN'T ELIMINATE MINE BESIDES, THE ONLY MAKE ME REALIZE HOW INFERIOR I AM
SHIT MAN, YKNOW WE'RE ALL GONNA DIE, AND WHETHER WE'RE DE-PRESSED OR HAPPY IT AWT GONNA MAKE MUCH DIFFERENG
THE NEXT DAY
HAPPY FEELS BETTER TO ME!
I'M SICK OF THIS
I'M GOING TO END IT ALL!
GO AHEAD, YOU ASSHOLE, YOU SHOULD'VE NEVER BEEN BORN!

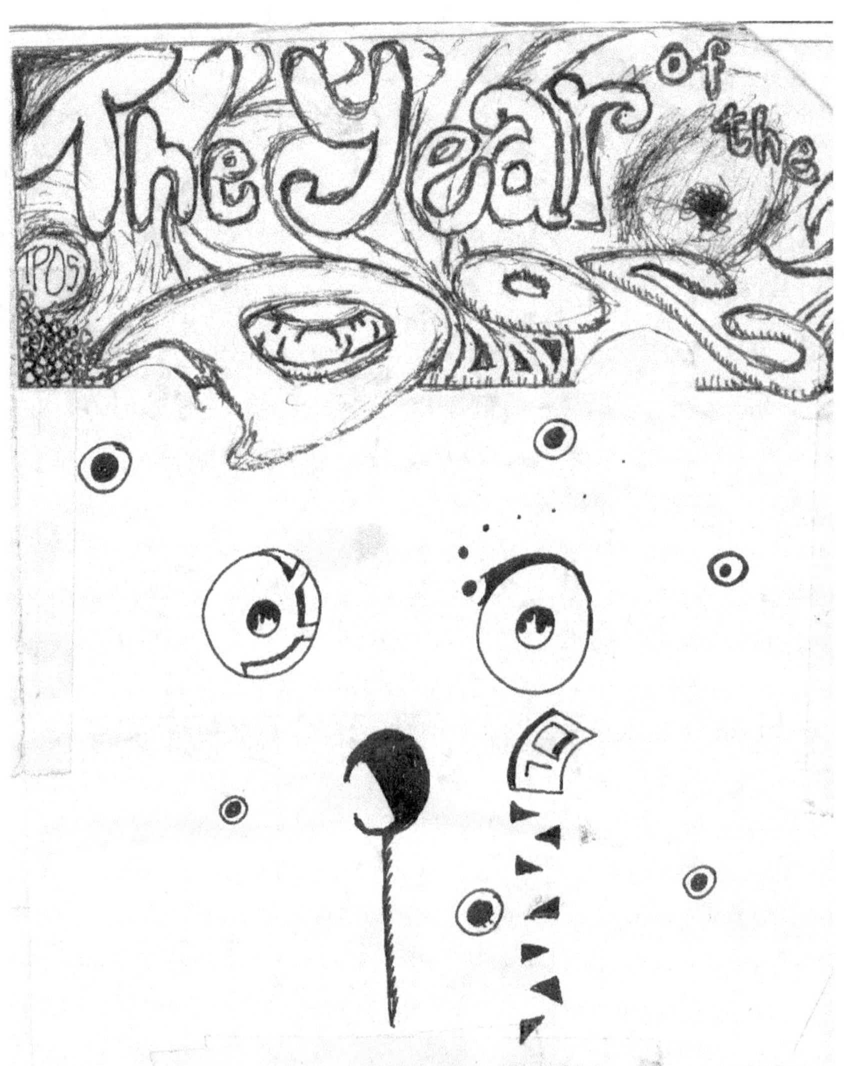

The Year
of the
the
1905

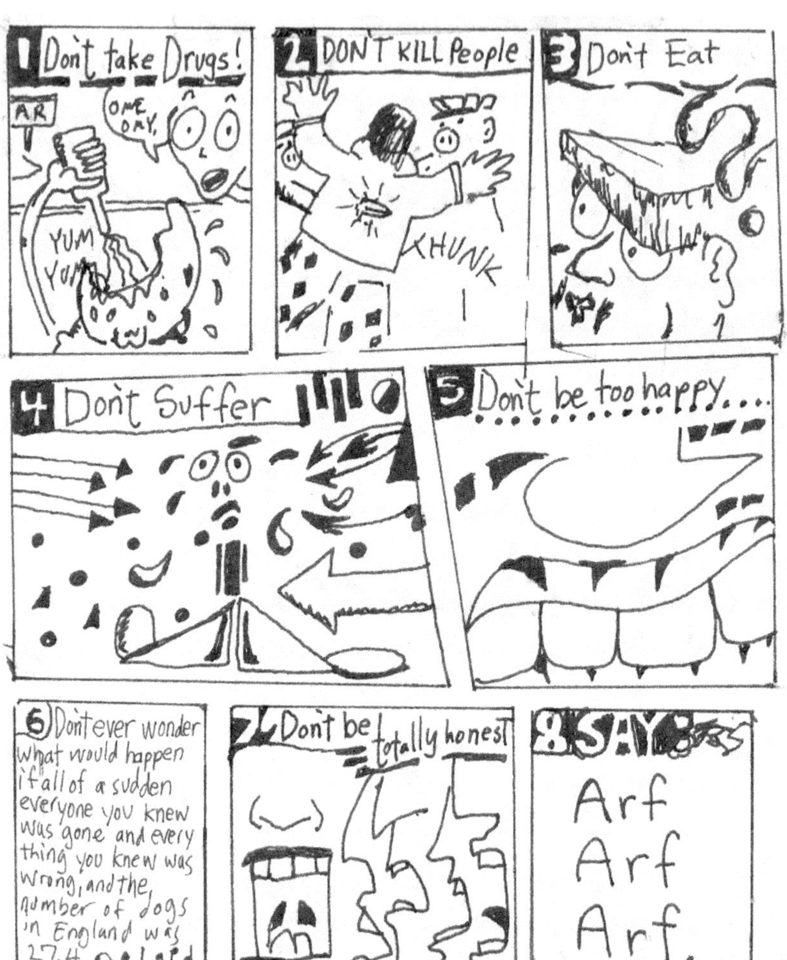

1) Don't take Drugs!
AR
ONE DAY,
YUM YUM
2) DON'T KILL People
KHUNK
3) Don't Eat
4) Don't Suffer
5) Don't be too happy....
6) Don't ever wonder what would happen if all of a sudden everyone you knew was gone and every thing you knew was wrong, and the number of dogs in England was 27.4. ~oLqPd
7) Don't be totally honest
8) SAY
Arf
Arf
Arf.

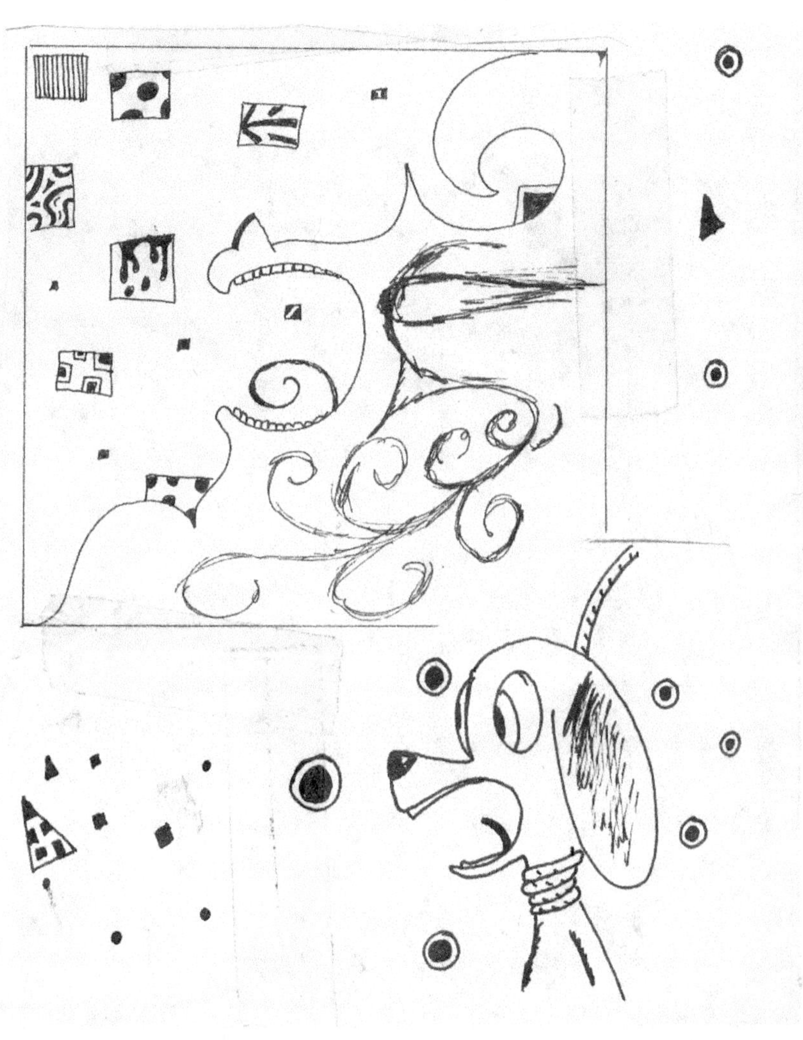

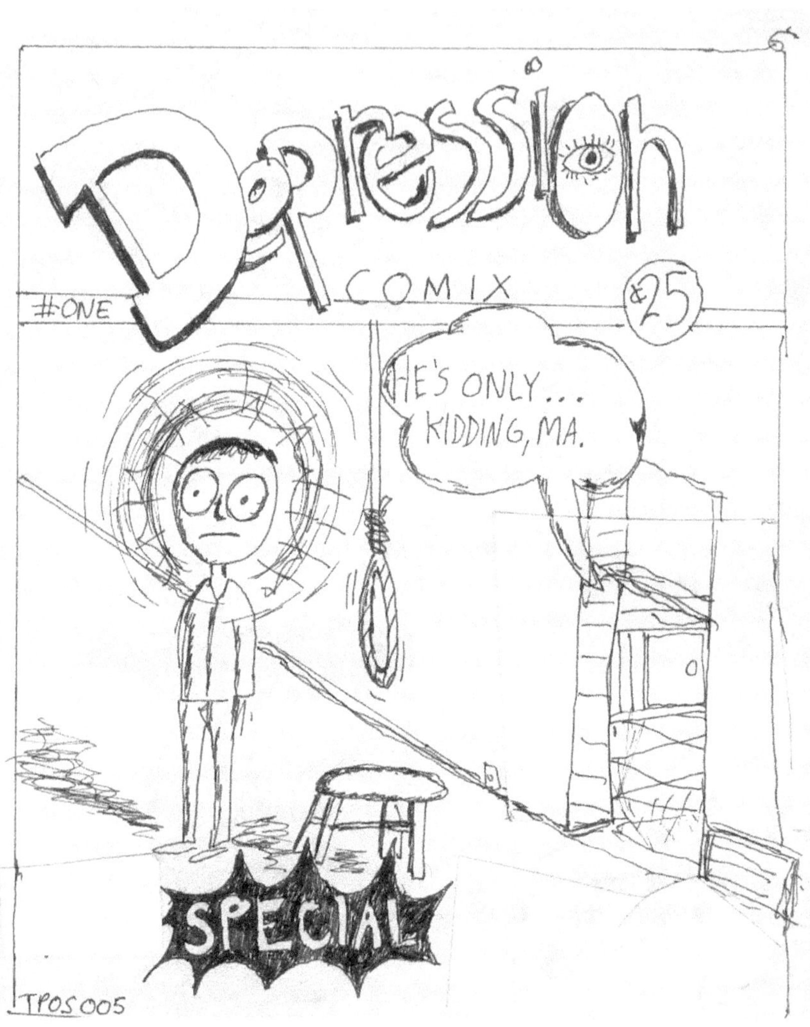

Depression
COMIX
#ONE
¢25
HE'S ONLY...
KIDDING, MA.
SPECIAL
TPOS005

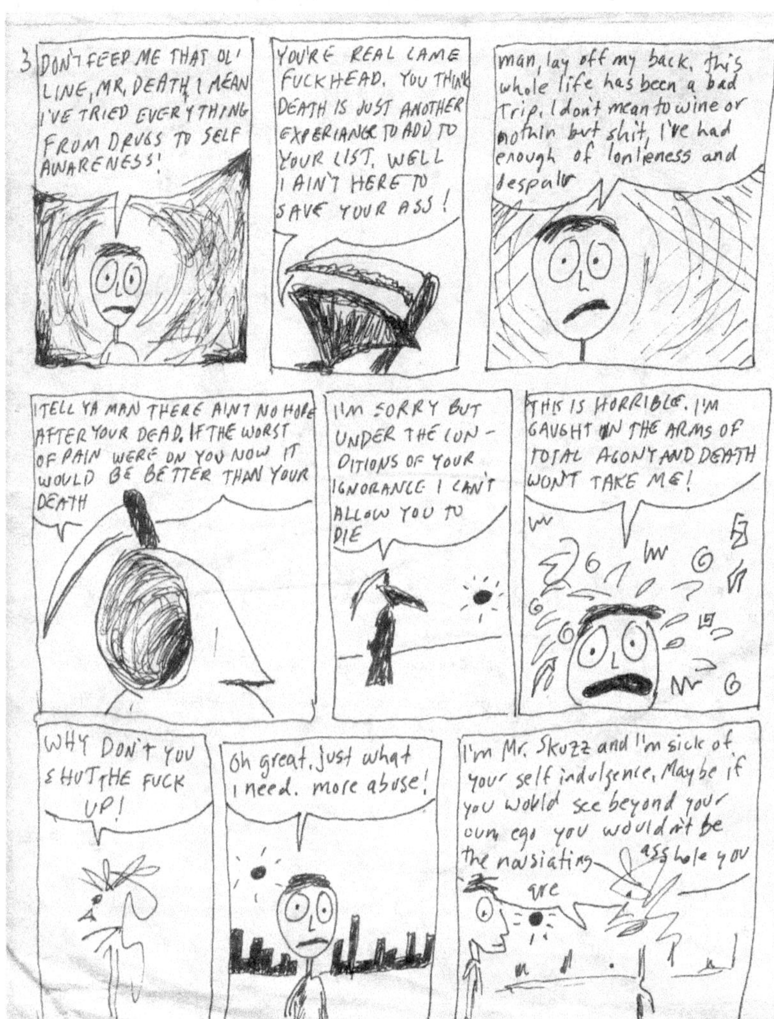

3 DON'T FEED ME THAT OL' LINE, MR. DEATH I MEAN I'VE TRIED EVERYTHING FROM DRUGS TO SELF AWARENESS!
YOU'RE REAL LAME FUCKHEAD. YOU THINK DEATH IS JUST ANOTHER EXPERIANCE TO ADD TO YOUR LIST. WELL I AIN'T HERE TO SAVE YOUR ASS!
man, lay off my back, this whole life has been a bad trip, I don't mean to wine or nothin but shit, I've had enough of lonleness and despair
I TELL YA MAN THERE AIN'T NO HOPE AFTER YOUR DEAD. IF THE WORST OF PAIN WERE ON YOU NOW IT WOULD BE BETTER THAN YOUR DEATH
I'M SORRY BUT UNDER THE CONDITIONS OF YOUR IGNORANCE I CAN'T ALLOW YOU TO DIE
THIS IS HORRIBLE. I'M CAUGHT IN THE ARMS OF TOTAL AGONY AND DEATH WON'T TAKE ME!
WHY DON'T YOU SHUT THE FUCK UP!
Oh great, just what I need. more abuse!
I'm Mr. Skuzz and I'm sick of your self indulgence, May be if you would see beyond your own ego you wouldn't be the nausiating asshole you are

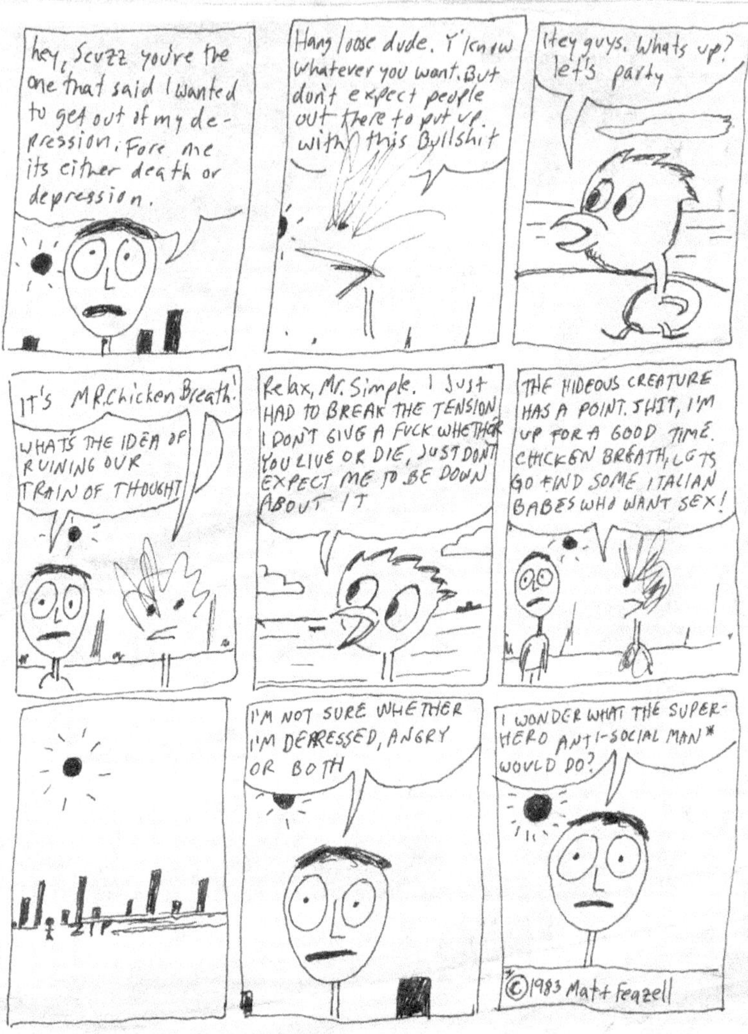

hey, Scuzz you're the one that said I wanted to get out of my depression. Fore me its either death or depression.
Hang loose dude. I'knew whatever you want. But don't expect people out there to put up with this Bullshit
Hey guys. Whats up? let's party
IT's MR. Chicken Breath! WHAT'S THE IDEA OF RUINING OUR TRAIN OF THOUGHT
Relax, Mr. Simple. I just had to break the tension I don't give a fuck whether you live or die, just dont expect me to be down about it
THE HIDEOUS CREATURE HAS A POINT. SHIT, I'M UP FOR A GOOD TIME. CHICKEN BREATH, LETS GO FIND SOME ITALIAN BABES WHO WANT SEX!
I'M NOT SURE WHETHER I'M DEPRESSED, ANGRY OR BOTH
I WONDER WHAT THE SUPER-HERO ANTI-SOCIAL MAN * WOULD DO?
©1983 Matt Feazell

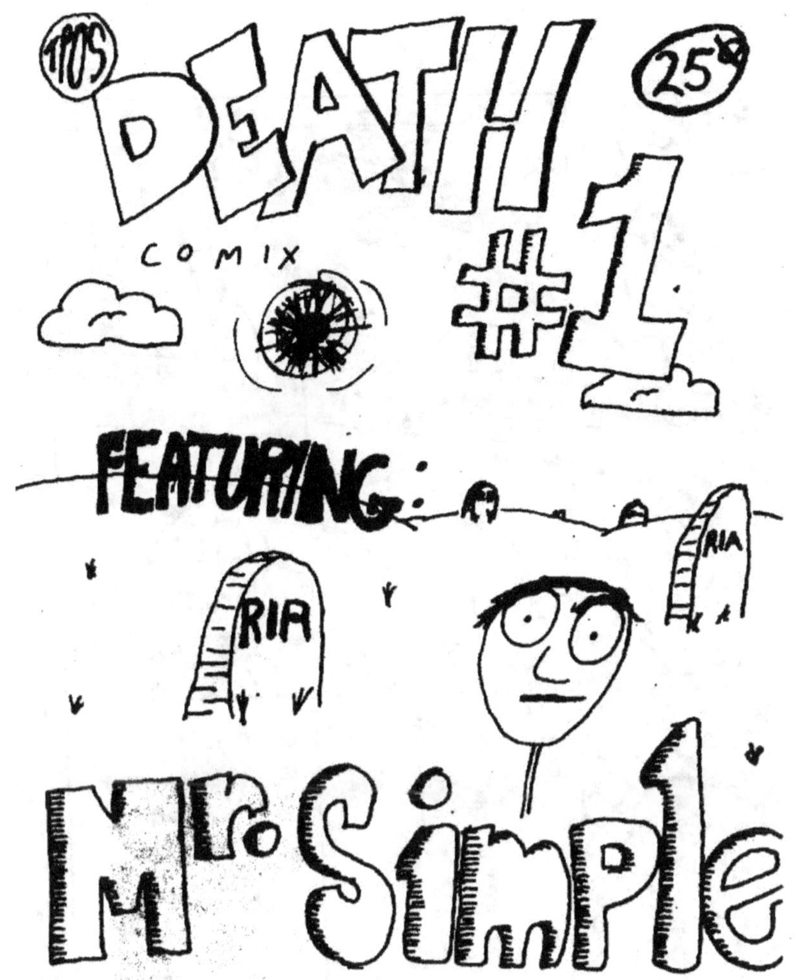

TAOS
25¢
DEATH
COMIX
#1.
FEATURING:
R.I.A
R.I.A
Mr. Simple

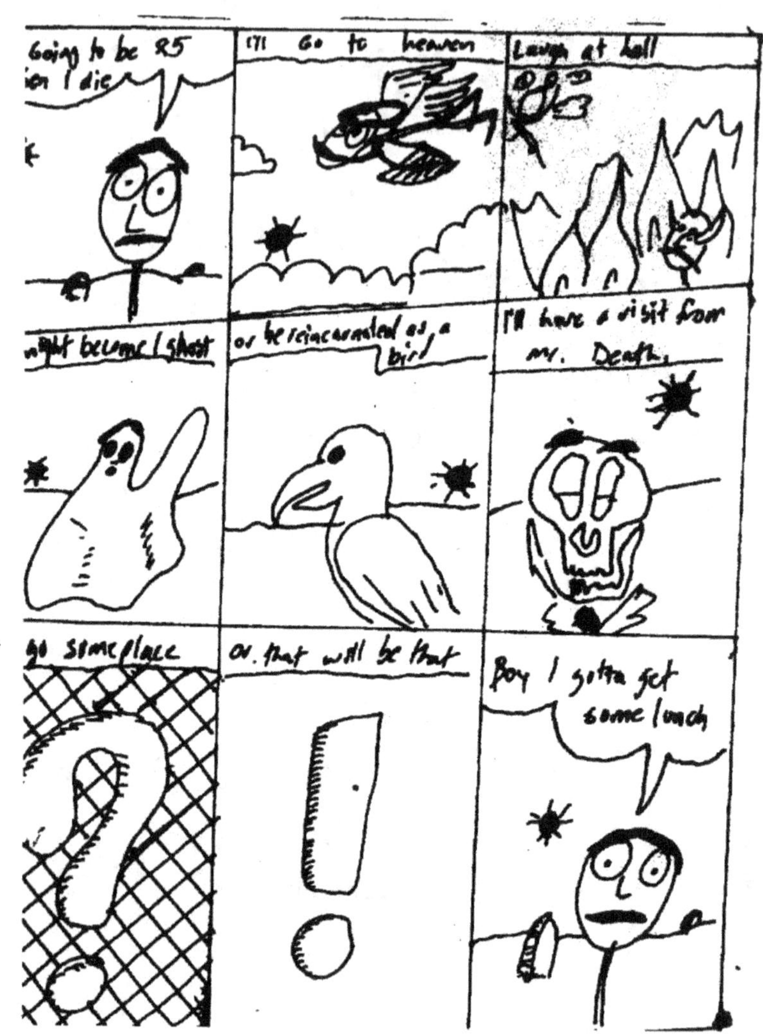
Going to be 85 when I die
I'll go to heaven
Laugh at hell
might become a ghost
or be reincarnated as a bird
I'll have a visit from Mr. Death.
go someplace
or that will be that
Boy I gotta get some lunch

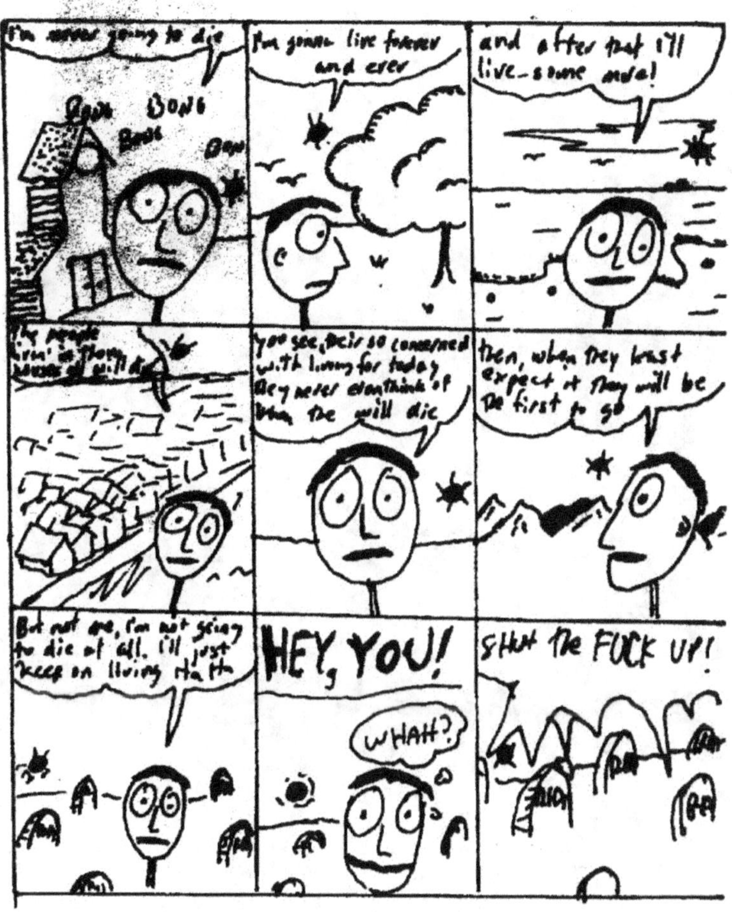

I'm never going to die
I'm gonna live forever and ever
and after that I'll live some more!
BONG BONG BONG BONG
My people livin' in them houses will die
you see, their so concerned with living for today, they never eventhink of when the will die
then, when they least expect it they will be the first to go
But not me, I'm not going to die at all. I'll just keep on living ha ha
HEY, YOU!
WHAH?
SHUT the FUCK UP!

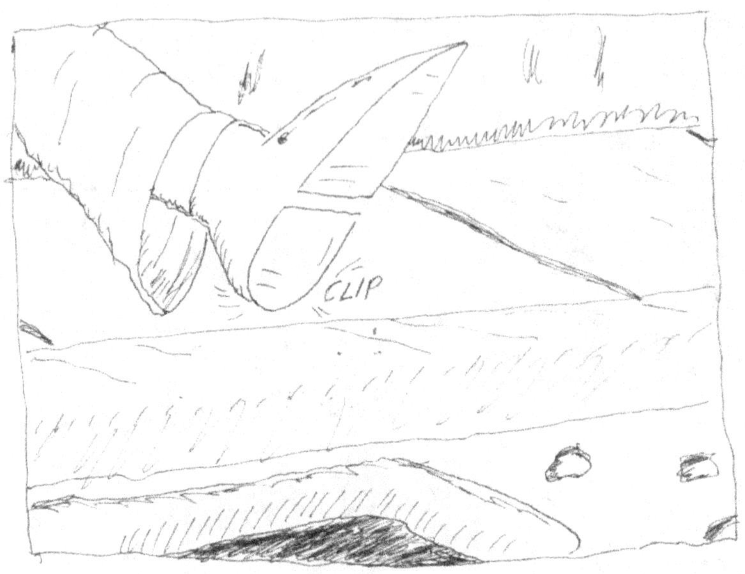

CLIP

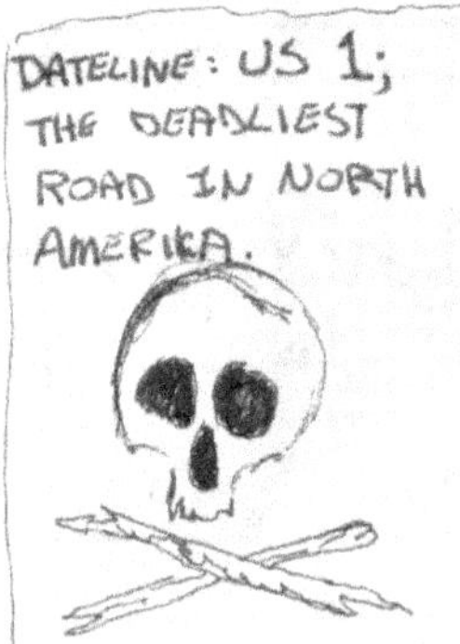

DATELINE: US 1;
THE DEADLIEST
ROAD IN NORTH
AMERICA.

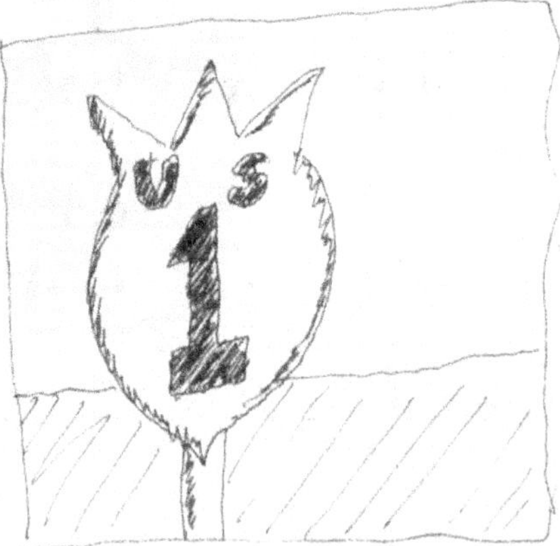

US
1

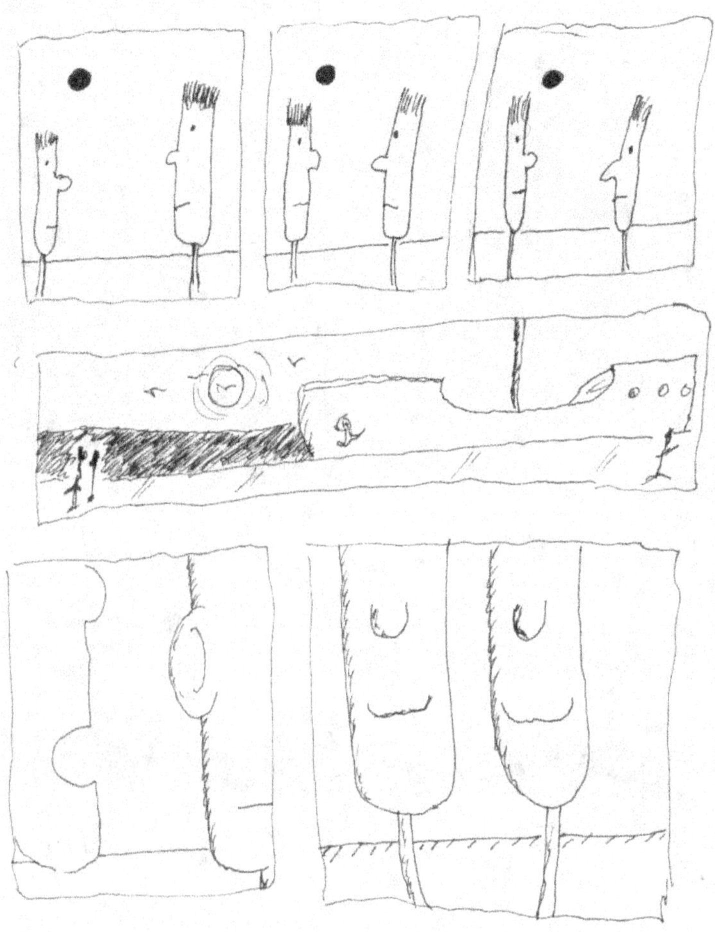

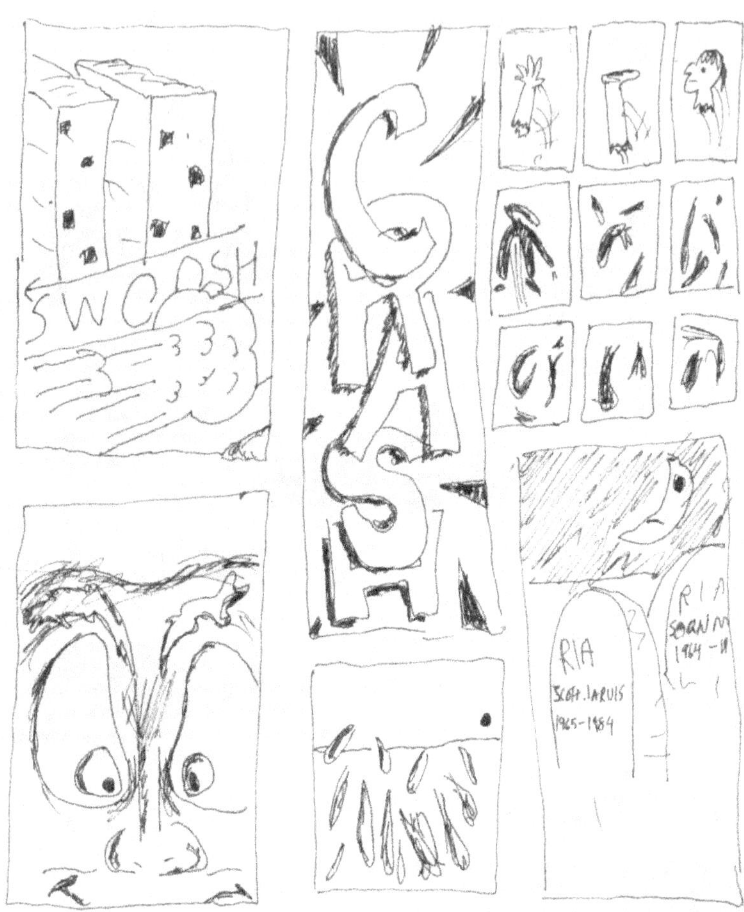

SWOOSH
CRASH
RIA
SCOTT JARVIS
1965-1984
RIA
SEAN M
1964 - 84

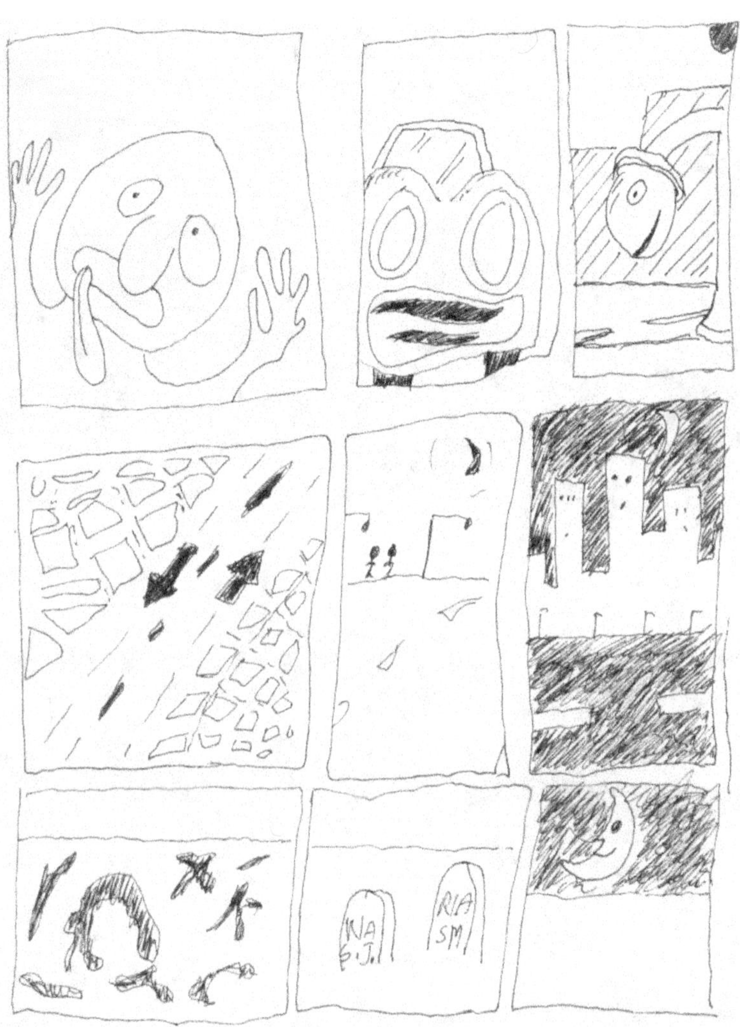
NA
P.J.
RIA
SM

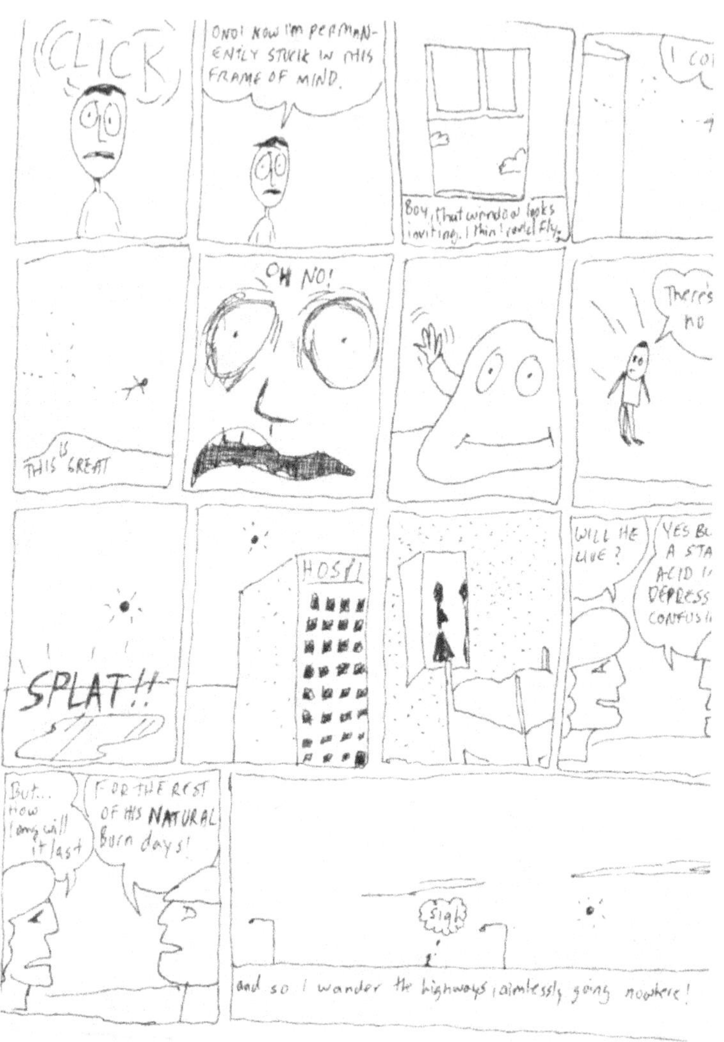
(CLICK)
ONO! NOW I'm PERMAN- ENTLY STUCK IN THIS FRAME OF MIND.
Boy, that window looks inviting. I think I could fly.
I CO
THIS IS GREAT
OH NO!
There's no
SPLAT!!
HOSP
WILL HE LIVE?
YES B.. A STA.. ACID I.. DEPRESS.. CONFUS..
But... How long will it last?
FOR THE REST OF HIS NATURAL BORN DAYS!
sigh
and so I wander the highways, aimlessly, going nowhere!

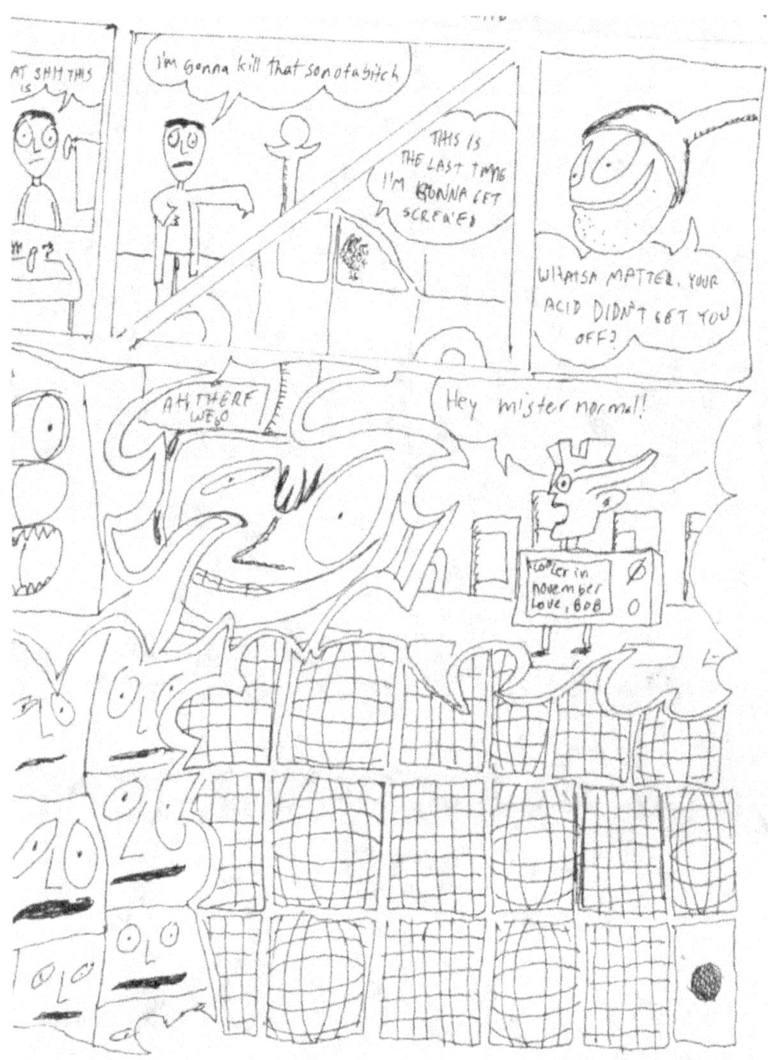
AT SHH THIS IS
I'm gonna kill that sonofabitch
THIS IS THE LAST TIME I'M GONNA GET SCREWED
WHATSA MATTER, YOUR ACID DIDN'T GET YOU OFF?
AH, THERE WE GO
Hey mister normal!
come in november love, BOB

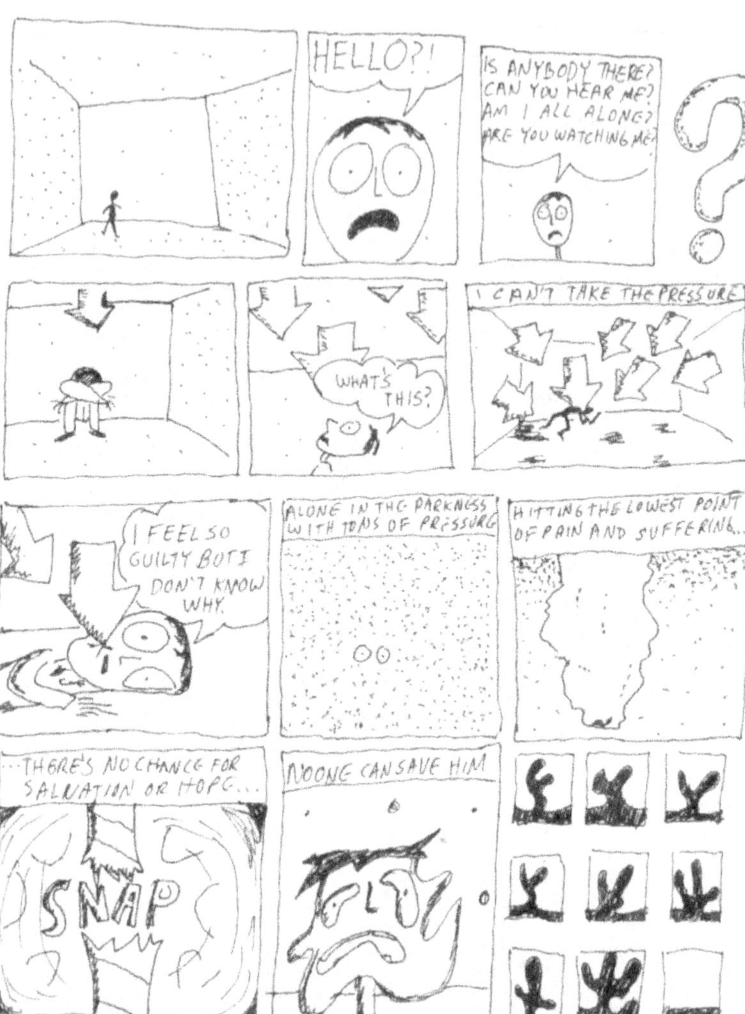

HELLO?!
IS ANYBODY THERE? CAN YOU HEAR ME? AM I ALL ALONE? ARE YOU WATCHING ME?
WHAT'S THIS?
I CAN'T TAKE THE PRESSURE
I FEEL SO GUILTY BUT I DON'T KNOW WHY.
ALONE IN THE DARKNESS WITH TONS OF PRESSURE
HITTING THE LOWEST POINT OF PAIN AND SUFFERING...
...THERE'S NO CHANCE FOR SALVATION OR HOPE...
SNAP
NOONE CAN SAVE HIM

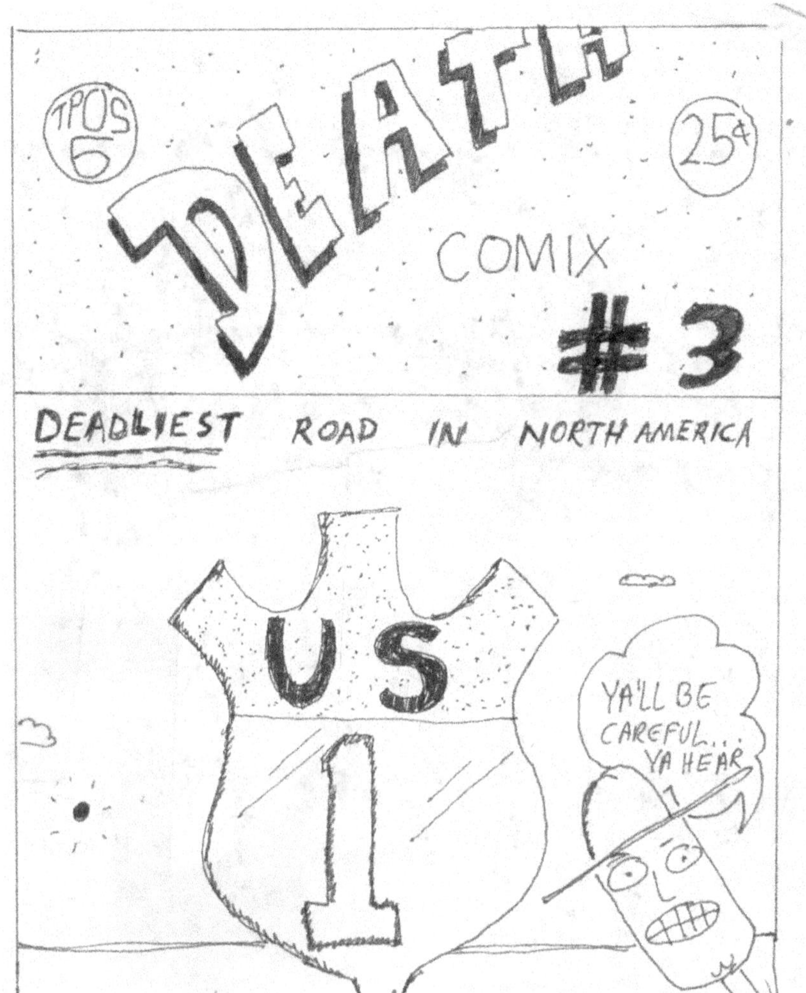

TPOS 6
25¢
DEATH
COMIX
#3
DEADLIEST ROAD IN NORTH AMERICA
US
1
YA'LL BE CAREFUL... YA HEAR

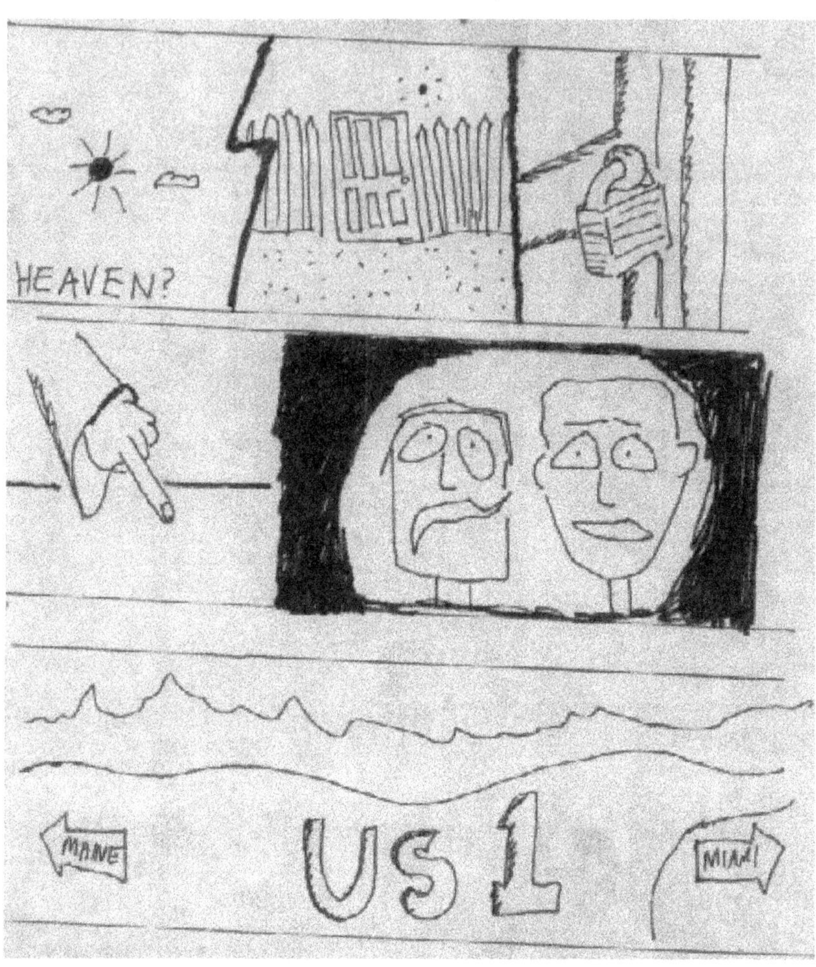

HEAVEN?
MANE
US 1
MIAMI

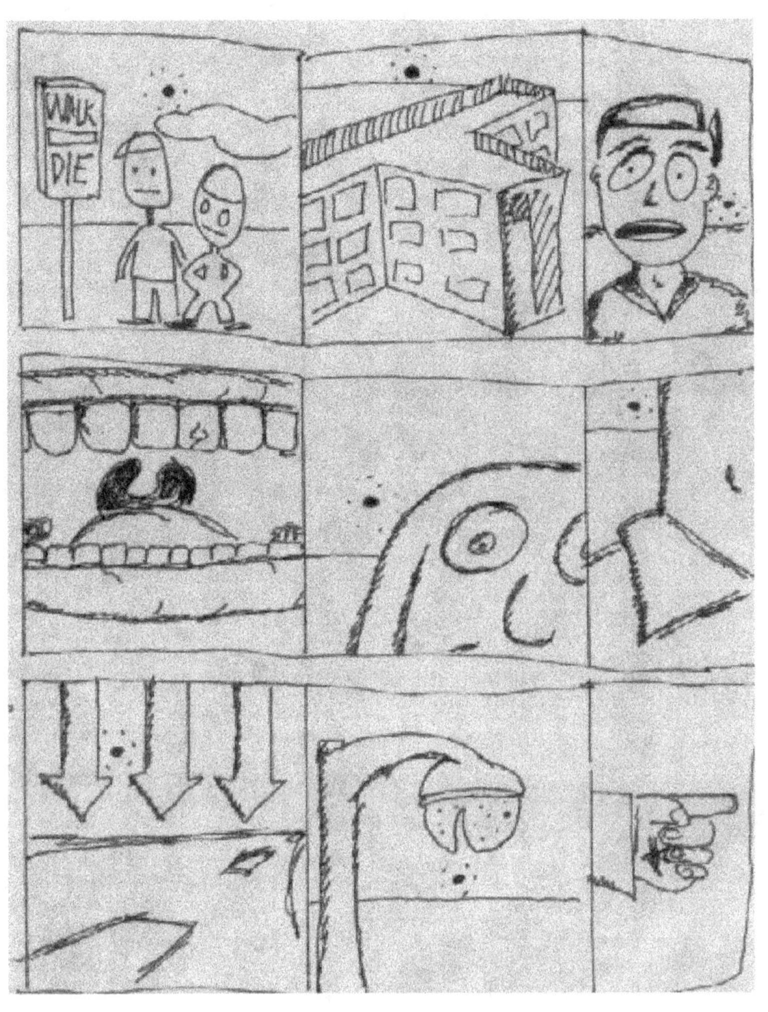

WALK
DIE